Data-Based Decision Making and Dynamic Planning:

A School Leader's Guide

Paul G. Preuss

EYE ON EDUCATION
6 DEPOT WAY WEST, SUITE 106
LARCHMONT, NY 10538
(914) 833–0551
(914) 833–0761 fax
www.eyeoneducation.com

Library of Congress Cataloging-in-Publication Data

Preuss, Paul G., 1942-
Data-based decision making and dynamic planning, A school leader's guide / Paul G. Preuss.
      p. cm.
   Includes bibliographical references.
ISBN 978-1-59667-070-9
1. Educational planning—United States. 2. Decision making—United States. 3. School management and organization—United States. I. Title.
LA210.P675 2008
371.2—dc22

2007038446

10 9 8 7 6 5 4 3 2 1

Meet the Author

Dr. Paul G. Preuss has completed 36 years of service in the public schools of New York State as teacher, principal, superintendent, and as assistant Board of Cooperative Educational Services (BOCES) superintendent. He coauthored the unified Planning Process, which served as a basis for New York's Comprehensive District Education Planning process (CDEP), and established and directed the New York State Technical Assistance Center for Comprehensive District Education Planning. He served as a member and co-chair of the New York State CDEP Steering Committee and the Steering Committee of the New York State Data Analysts Group. Dr. Preuss has authored the "School Leader's Guide to Root Cause Analysis: Using Data to Dissolve Problems." In retirement he has provided consulting and training services to school districts both locally and nationally.

Dr. Preuss holds degrees from Muhlenberg College, Colgate University, and Syracuse University. He is a student of organizational behavior and has become a systems thinker. His work is backed by 32 years of administrative experience in making positive things happen for students.

Acknowledgments

Most recently and immediately I wish to acknowledge, and thank, the critical readers of my working draft for their great care in pointing out areas that needed to be strengthened, areas that needed to be clarified, and areas that could be expressed more briefly. Sean Brady pointed out the need for me to better explain the role of data-based decision making. Victoria Bernhardt has always been a source of encouragement when I have needed it most. Diane Stultz suggested many improvements and helped to focus my thoughts on value-added analysis. In addition, thankfully, they pointed out the unique concepts contained within this text that enabled its publication.

Robert Sickles has been a very patient publisher during my struggles to find the necessary framework upon which my ideas and experiences could be organized. During these last few months in preparing the final draft he has provided both encouragement and professional guidance that has enhanced my ability to polish the final product.

If the goal of all educators is to instill within their students the ability to become lifelong learners, and if indeed that goal has been only partially realized within me, I still have so many people, institutions, and sources to acknowledge for what I share in this text that these acknowledgments should continue for many pages. For what I have written in the pages that follow comes from the processing of my experiences as a student, teacher, principal, superintendent, facilitator, presenter, colleague, trainer, reader, listener, and observer. It is through these accumulated hundreds upon hundreds of interactions with others, with and within different contexts, and with different media, that I have learned and then synthesized what I am attempting to pass on to those who read these pages. Suffice it to say that I owe a great deal to my many colleagues and to all who are on the same journey of improving educational systems for all our students. We have all touched each other as we continue our travels on this same path.

Table of Contents

1
Introduction: The Context and Overview

Over the fifty-eight years that I have been engaged in public education, as a student or professionally, I have observed or taken part in several fundamental shifts in national educational policy. Each wave of reform washed over the educational establishment as a Tsunami, creating major streams of action as well as backwaters of inaction or delayed action. Each of these shifts created its own bureaucracy and established new operational rules for educators. Each came with new terminology, concepts and acronyms. Each shift required a steep learning curve until it became more fully integrated into the ongoing process of public education.

On May 17, 1954 The United States Supreme Court issued its decision in the *Brown vs. Board of Education* case "that in the field of public education the doctrine of 'separate but equal' has no place. Separate educational facilities are inherently unequal. Therefore, we hold that the plaintiffs and others similarly situated for whom the actions have been brought are, by reason of the segregation complained of, deprived of the equal protection of the laws guaranteed by the Fourteenth Amendment." This was the first major wave of recent reform. In 1957 President Eisenhower sent troops to Little Rock, Arkansas to enforce the Supreme Court's school desegregation order. In that same year the first Civil Rights Act in 79 years was passed in Congress and signed into law. The battle for equal rights for all continues to this day.

The second of these waves was the *National Defense Education Act* (NDEA) of 1958 which was the federal government's response to the 1957 orbiting of Sputnik I by the Russians. The fact that the Russians had beaten the United States in orbiting a satellite was seen as prima fascia proof that we lagged in science and mathematics. NDEA's primary focus was the support of stronger education in science, mathematics, and foreign language at all levels of learning, public school through university. NDEA marked the first time that the federal government took such massive steps to support education and it contained specific

1

prohibitions blocking any attempt to federally control local administration, curriculum, or instruction. NDEA began the progression of federal programs in support of education which, over time, became increasingly regulatory.

The third was Title IX, of the educational amendments enacted in 1972 that required that "No person in the United States shall, on the basis of sex, be excluded from participation in, be denied the benefits of, or be subjected to discrimination under any education program or activity receiving Federal financial assistance." One of the larger impacts of Title IX was on the development of vastly larger sports programs for girls and women and an increase in the variety of educational access for both males and females. Of course there were many other educational dislocations brought about by Title IX and our country today is once again substantially different because of it.

The fourth was the 1975 passage in Congress of Public Law 94-142 which is now called the *Individuals with Disabilities Act* (IDEA). Again federal funding was used as a lever to require each state to develop and implement plans and policies to "assure a free appropriate public education to all children with disabilities." Once again, our country and its schools are substantially different today as a result of this law.

The fifth fundamental shift was the growth of teacher unions that took place across the country during the 1960s. By 1970 more than half of all U.S. teachers were members of either the National Education Association (NEA) or of the American Federation of Teachers (AFT). In the wake of increased membership came increased political clout and in many states collective bargaining was written into law. Today the clout of unionized teachers politically and educationally is substantial.

The sixth and most recent fundamental shift is the greatly increased demand that schools be held accountable for student learning and that such student learning will be assessed in a standardized manner and reported to the public at least on an annual basis. Although many state education departments were moving in this direction, the movement became an avalanche upon the January 8, 2002 signing of the No Child Left Behind (NCLB) Federal legislation by President Bush. This most recent reauthorization of the 1965 Elementary and Secondary Education Act (ESEA) is built upon four major initiatives:

♦ Strong accountability for results

♦ More freedom for states and communities

♦ The use of proven educational methods, and

♦ Providing more choice to parents

NCLB requires that all students be assessed in reading and math each year in grades 3 through 8 and at least once in high school. Based upon the results of these assessments schools not making Adequate Yearly Progress (AYP) are identified as Schools in Need of Improvement (SINI). Details regarding the complexity of NCLB are best found at: http://www.ed.gov/nclb/overview/ as it is not my intent to dwell on its specifics but rather on its implications for educational leaders and for all those concerned with improving student learning.

While the causes for this sixth shift are multiple, the root causes can be grouped into a category called "economic ramifications of the global market place." We, as a nation, can no longer tolerate allowing a third of our students to leave high school without the basic skills to function and compete in the world marketplace. Once upon a time, perhaps even in their parent's lifetimes, there was sufficient room for them on the lowest rungs of our economic ladder—no longer. Thomas L. Freidman's book: *The World is Flat* best captures both the context and urgency for this belated reformation of America's schools It is in the midst of this sixth fundamental shift that this text is being written and it is upon the required use of data in response to this latest shift that its content is focused.

From the practitioner's point of view there are several key processes that have been made necessary by NCLB. These include:

♦ The use of data to measure student learning and program effectiveness

♦ Public accountability for student learning by reporting out the data

♦ Organizational and professional consequences for student failure to learn

♦ The use of student learning data to improve learning results

♦ Databased Decision Making

Schools now find that they are not only required to amass and use large amounts of student learning data but that this data must be used to inform instruction, parents, *and* the general public. Each school building and school district is required to issue an annual "report card" showing the degree of learner and cohort proficiency in at least the areas of math and English language. Failure to meet required goals or failure to meet annual yearly progress toward these goals result in consequences for the building or district and/or its leadership and staff.

As with each of the previous waves of educational change, there have been states and districts that are well down the road toward implementation while other states and districts ranged anywhere from close to far behind. As these first adopters rapidly moved forward, the gap between them and the last adopters grew larger. As a result we now have a full spectrum of data-enabled and accountable schools, districts, and states. Although this variety among states, districts, and schools appears as a patchwork quilt of programs and processes—some complete, some incomplete, and others yet to be started—it is obvious that the national trend since the signing of NCLB is forever increasing the knowledgeable use of data to inform decisions about improving student learning and for providing system accountability to stakeholders.

This morning's edition of the *Glens Falls Post-Star* (2006, Nov. 11) contained an article about the Roman Catholic Diocese of Albany, NY, schools "developing an on-line system that will allow parents to check their children's attendance records, grades, homework, and classroom schedules." Of course teachers and administrators will also have access to this information. The program being used is the "Pearson School System's Powerschool," which is reported as being used in 7,800 schools across the country (see: http://www.powerschool.com/). Across the nation there are many other programs and processes that enable schools and districts to accomplish similar things.

It is hoped that:

- Teachers and administrators have been trained to the point of proficiency in order to make use of this tool.

- The system has committed to making databased decisions

- Parents have been trained to the point of proficiency

- Parents have the ability to go online in their homes

- The system has provided sufficient additional trained staff to oversee and maintain the system.

- The tool becomes established within the culture and norms of the diocesan schools to the extent that it becomes a regular way to do business rather than just one more add-on or passing fad.

One can hardly imagine our schools or nation today without the influence of the previous five fundamental shifts. In the not too distant future it will be equally difficult to imagine our schools or nation without the influence of educational data, educational accountability, and educational data-driven decision making. This sixth wave is upon us and remains the focus of this text.

At the risk of being too brief, my intent is to provide school district personnel with sufficient depth of understanding to be able to process the concepts and skills of data, databased decision making and dynamic planning without belaboring them. In this way I hope that this text serves as a relatively quick and easy "in-the-trenches" handbook for all those engaged in school improvement. Over the past few years many educators have become increasingly better informed regarding the proper use of data to improve student learning and I trust that this text can build upon that base. While there are also an increasing array of resources lined up to serve schools in need of improvement, there are also few conceptual overviews of how to place all of this activity within the context of an operating school system. This text was written with the hope of filling that void and providing the overview necessary for successful implementation of a dynamic and productive school improvement effort.

The concepts within this text are based upon the my 31 years as a school administrator; my coauthoring of the *Unified Planning Processes*; my experiences as the Co-Chair of the New York State Comprehensive District Education Planning Steering Committee (CDEP); as Director of the New York State Center for Comprehensive Planning; and upon my experiences in training, consulting with, and facilitating the planning process in schools across New York and other states.

The chapters that follow are sequenced in a linear and logical manner but with the caveat that very little in the today's world of public education remains logical and/or linear. Each chapter is related both to what precedes and proceeds it—hence all of the text's content is linked in other than a linear manner. It is much more a web of understandings confined within the linear boundaries of our language and its means of transmittal – the linear sentence and book. So feel free to bounce around the text as you desire. No doubt you will find all that you require by the end of your journey. The pages that follow make my case for databased decision making and dynamic planning for districts, schools, and classrooms.

Chapter 2 introduces the concept of Databased Decision Making and the essential concepts related to its success. It includes a model illustrating the various kinds of data and how they are used together to convert data to wisdom.

Chapter 3 deals with a concept I developed in 2004 that I have called "Data Pathways." It is my attempt to explain the many ways in which educational data can and is being used to inform decision making and how many individual data sets are needed to transform data to information, information to knowledge, knowledge to understanding, and understanding to wisdom.

Chapter 4 focuses upon the relatively new process of using student proficiency data to compute annual student progress. This process is referred to as "value-added analysis" as it computes the amount of learning (progress) that has occurred within a student over time that can be directly attributed to the "value-added" actions of school.

Chapter 5 explains the key concepts of: Data-Driven Decision Making, Systems Thinking, Key Indicators of Student Success, and Root Cause Analysis. Understanding and making use of these concepts is essential for the success of all school improvement efforts.

In Chapter 6 I explain what I have come to believe must become the culmination of all that has been covered in Chapters 1 through 5—and that is a truly Dynamic Planning process. Dynamic Planning is a process of planning that is no longer annular but instead becomes a consistent aspect of all processes within the school. It is the way the school goes about its business and, of course, it includes data and data-driven decision making. Although the term is certainly not original with me, I found over 113,000 Google hits in 0.13 seconds, it is the term that I believe best describes the vision I am attempting to share. One writer called it "planning on the fly" and I suppose there is a simple truth to that, but there is more, as you will see in Chapter 6.

Chapter 7 is an invitation to *Make It Happen: The Crucial Step in Creating* a truly databased, results-oriented planning process for the district, school, program, or classroom and contains a listing of 18 components, or tasks, involved in getting started toward full incorporation of Databased Decision Making and Dynamic Planning. Each of these tasks is discussed briefly.

Within the text I have identified additional resources for those who want to explore various items further. The Bibliography has been purposefully limited to those few texts that I have found most meaningful out of respect for the demands upon the reader's precious time. A Glossary and listing of acronyms has been prepared to add clarity.

Hopefully, my goal to provide a brief but sufficient guide for "in-the-trenches" educators on the concepts and skills necessary for successful implementation of databased decision making and dynamic planning have been realized within the following pages.

2

Data and Databased Decision Making

In the Introduction I wrote of the sixth fundamental wave of reform in education: the demand that schools become accountable for student learning. This wave has greatly increased the necessity for and the use of data. Like each of the previous five waves, the sixth wave has brought new vocabulary as descriptors for numerous new concepts. Databased Decision Making (DBDM) is one of the larger concepts to emerge from this shift. A similar term used to describe the same concept is Data-Driven Decision Making (D3M).

Both terms were "googled" as part of my preparation for writing this chapter. Google identified 194,000 citations for Databased Decision Making and 95,500 citations for Data-Driven Decision Making. A smaller number of references were found for Management by Fact and most of those were associated with business applications. The first hundred citations for each term were reviewed and I found that the context for over 80% of all citations for DBDM and D3M was education. As far as I am concerned, the terms can be used interchangeably. But what is Databased Decision Making? Listed in the Additional Resources section at the end of this chapter are multiple explanations that I have found. Each item is referenced with an Internet site to identify both the source and resource for obtaining deeper knowledge of the concept.

In reviewing these 19 items it is obvious that in general, they are in conceptual agreement. The variety amongst them is in the complexity of their explanation and their definition for the process of DBDM. In fact, some offer no definition but rely only on their description of the process.

Perhaps among the simplest are: Judy Salpeter's[1] to collect, manage, analyze, and learn from a wide array of data"; the definition presented by the Na-

---

1 The journal, "TechLearning" (*www.techlearning.com*) has provided a rich array of information on DBDM over the last several years. In the March 2004 issue, Judy Salpeter, in her article on "Data Mining with a Mission" provides the following simple definition of DBDM: "there is no denying that an integral part of the business of K-12 education today is to collect, manage, analyze, and learn from a wide array of data". The June 2002 issue

tional Study for School Evaluation (NSSE)[2] is "using data that are gathered on a regular basis (and additional information, as needed) to inform planning, decision making, and reporting activities"; Denis P. Doyle's[3] D3M "is the process of collecting student data—academic performance, attendance, demographics, etc.—in such a way that administrators, teachers and parents can accurately as-

---

contains an informative article by Todd McIntire entitled: "The Administrator's Guide to Data-Driven Decision Making. Click on "Data Management" on the home page "Hot Topics" button and 16 different articles appear, two of which are by Todd McIntire on the topic of data mining (June and April 2005 issues).

2 Parents for Public Schools (www.parents4publicschools.com) reported in its November 2001 issue of "Parent Press" that The National Study for School Evaluation (www.NSSE. org) developed a framework for Data-Driven Decision Making that includes the following four elements: Mining Data, collecting and managing relevant information on performance and school characteristics; Analyzing Data, evaluating the data to create knowledge through comparisons, relationships, patterns, and trends; Communicating Data, making sense of the data for educators, parents, community members, and policy makers; Using Data, maximizing the role of data in school improvement planning.
eScholar (www.escholar.com) reports on the following 1998 NSSE definition of data-driven decision making: "using data that are gathered on a regular basis (and additional information, as needed) to inform planning, decision making, and reporting activities." They continue that "data-driven decision making activities fall into the following four categories: mining the data—collecting and managing data; analyzing the data—to transfer data into information, knowledge, understanding, and wisdomG; communicating the data—reporting to essential customer groups; and using the data by maximizing the role of data in school improvement planning."

3 Denis P. Doyle provides this definition: data-driven decision making "is the process of collecting student data—academic performance, attendance, demographics, etc.—in such a way that administrators, teachers and parents can accurately assess student learning. They can then make decisions based on the data to improve administrative and instructional systems to continually promote student achievement. (Doyl, Denis P., May 2003.

sess student learning"; and that written by Jim Cox,[4] "A data-driven organization is one that uses information, collected formally or informally, every step along the way."

Each of these simple definitions is fine to a certain point, but each also lacks completeness. Salpeter's provides no explanation of what actions will take place after collecting, managing, analyzing, and learning. I sense that the NSSE definition lacks something, perhaps a pinch of salt necessary to explain in greater detail the term "using." Doyle's definition leaves me with the necessity of asking what actions are going to be taken following the accurate assessment of student learning, or is assessment of learning the end point of the process? I have to confess that I think Jim Cox's is my favorite because it covers a lot of ground, especially the words "every step along the way." I would have liked to see him insert the word "all" between uses and information. Perhaps my favoritism is the result of his words, which accompany his definition when he mentions the importance of beliefs and organizational climate to effective schools and the journey to be data-driven. Interestingly, none of these in their initial definitions mentions the primary purpose of improving student learning.

Some of the sources do not attempt to define DBDM but rather provide a description. One of the more complex descriptions is that provided by the Rand Corporation,[5] which covers nearly a full page of small type along with a sche-

---

Data-Driven Decision Making, *The Journal*) Denis P. Doyle can be reached at: denis@school net.c_Hlt161046475oBM_4_m (www.thedoylereport.com)

4 The Technology Information Center for Administrative Leadership (TICAL) is a very fine site containing many resources for those seeking to make use of technology in their school improvement efforts (*www.portical.org*). A simple 5-paragraph essay by consultant Jim Cox (January 26, 2007) concludes with the following: "A data-driven organization is one that uses information, collected formally or informally every step along the way. A data-driven organization continually asks, "Why?" and supplies answers with information rather than just with opinions." Jim Cox earlier mentions the importance of beliefs and organizational climate to effective schools and the journey to be data-driven.

5 The Rand Corporation website contains an 18 page 2006 occasional paper "Making Sense of Data-Driven Decision Making in Education" which deals with DDDM at the district, school & classroom levels which can be found at: *http://www.rand.org/ pubs/occasional_ papers/2006/ RAND_OP170.pdf*. The paper is based upon five Rand studies of schools making use of data. Their definition of DDDM covers nearly half a page and a schematic. Their description of the process includes gathering of data (input data, process data, outcome data, and satisfaction data) and converting it to information by a process of organizing the data and combined with an understanding of the context through a process of analysis. This information then becomes actionable knowledge through a process of applying judgments, weighting and prioritization. Actionable knowledge is then used to make decisions regarding the following issues: set and assess progress toward goals, address individual or group needs, evaluate effectiveness of practices, assess whether client needs are being met, reallocation of resources, enhance processes to improve outcomes.

matic that informs the narrative. Even though Rand's description is detailed, it does not cover what I believe to be the essence of DBDM. It is much like describing an airplane without saying that it can fly.

For me, the essential characteristics of DBDM are contained in the following relatively simple definition: DBDM is a system of deeply rooted beliefs, actions, and processes that infuses organizational culture and regularly organizes and transforms data to wisdom for the purpose of making organizational decisions.

As this definition is applied within this text, the organizations we are thinking about are school offices, classrooms, buildings, and districts. The decisions that we are most focused upon are those related to the improvement of student learning, progress, and achievement.

Let's look at this definition again, focusing on the nine essential components that are italicized here: DBDM is a *system* of *deeply rooted beliefs, actions,* and *processes* that *infuses organizational culture and regularly organizes and transforms data to wisdom for the purpose of making organizational decisions.*

DBDM is a system: The concept of systems is one of several "key concepts" covered in detail in Chapter 5. Suffice it to say now that DBDM is not an item, a singularity, an "add-on process" but rather it is a full-blown network of processes that connect broadly across the organization with all other processes. It is not an outrigger process—something on the bookshelf to be taken out and dusted off every 12 months. DBDM is a web of interconnections that is operative 24/7 all year long.

Deeply rooted beliefs: Leadership of the organization believes in the ultimate superiority of DBDM for all decision making, and staff within the organization has come to believe in the ultimate superiority of DBDM. DBDM has become part of the organization's culture and climate. The Board of Education, parents, and other publics have come to believe in the ultimate superiority of DBDM for decision making.

Deeply rooted actions: Most actions and all major actions of the organization come from the use of DBDM. It is the way the organization goes about its business. This text focuses on the improvement of student learning, however, DBDM is just as naturally used in organizational finance, transportation, food services, student discipline, and attendance, student health services, and so on. In fact, these other functions may have already been using DBDM for many years. DBDM becomes the most natural organizational and individual response to the need for a decision.

Deeply rooted processes: DBDM is embedded within the organization through a wide network of processes that both feed it with resources and allow it to inform decision making at all levels and in all corners of the system. A generic DBDM process will be shared later in this chapter as an example.

That infuses organizational culture: DBDM is the way the organization goes about its daily business. It is the way it recruits and hires and assigns staff, it is the way it evaluates programs, people, and results. It is a trusted, positive, focused organizational force for continuous improvement.

Regularly organizes and transforms data to wisdom: No actions should be taken on a single piece of data except to ask for more data. Data need to be triangulated with other data. To be effective DBDM must be able to transform data into information, information into knowledge, knowledge into understanding, and understanding into wisdom. This process of data transformation is covered in some detail in Chapter 5. The best decisions are made at the level of understanding and wisdom.

For the purpose of making organizational decisions: DBDM is not an annual event. It is a daily partner to nearly all key decision making within the organization. Of course, if there is a fire, pull the alarm or call 911. But after it is put out, examine why it took place, how it could have been avoided, and what actions must be taken to improve the future. If there is a staff member or program in need of immediate assistance, run and provide the necessary assistance. But then learn from the experience and reflect upon its cause and seek to remove its roots in order to eliminate or reduce the possibility of its happening again.

What does DBDM look like and how does it function within the organization? DBDM functions at a variety of levels: district, school, program, department, grade level, student cohorts, classroom, and individual students.

At the district level DBDM is perhaps most visible in the strategic planning process and is specifically used in the monitoring of student results and focusing resources on identified areas of need. This will look very different in the Montgomery (Maryland) County Schools (145,000 students, 199 school buildings) than it will in the Owen D. Young (New York) Central School (254 students, 1 school building). However, the function is the same—the collection and conversion of data to wisdom in support of making informed decisions that will enable improved learning. Examples of other district-level decisions that should be informed via DBDM processes include: school finance and taxation; staffing, including recruitment, hiring, tenuring, and staff assignment; food services; custodial; grounds and building maintenance; and transportation.

At the school building level we find many of the same processes that should benefit from DBDM. These include: monitoring of student achievement, student progress and building improvement plans, building budget, building staffing and supervision, student discipline, and student and staff attendance.

As one moves from the district level through the building level to the level of departments, programs, grade levels, and classrooms, the focus narrows from large groups of students and large cohorts of students to smaller groups of students, smaller cohorts, and down to individual students. At the level of departments, programs, and classrooms DBDM focuses more deeply on specific instructional issues such as: methods, materials, scheduling, content, and the needs of individual students.

Because DBDM should become infused throughout the organization and at many different levels, there is no single model that can be used to describe specifically what the process might look like. The example below is an attempt at using a simple generic model to explain the various components of DBDM.

Example of a Databased Decision-Making Model

1.	What is the issue at hand?	This could be a key indicator of student success (see Chapter 5); it could be something that has been identified as either a problem or something to be "fixed" or improved.
2.	What is the ideal condition?	What is the measurement used and what is considered to be the ideal level?
3.	What is the present condition?	Use the same metric as used above.
4.	What is the gap?	Simple gap analysis.
5.	Is this a priority issue?	This is a value judgment – if it is a priority issue, tackle it. If it is not a priority issue, place it on the back burner.
6.	Develop an "ends focused" goal statement.	The goal statement should explain: What is going to take place over what period of time using the data contained in items 2, 3, and 4 above.
7.	Search for root cause	Here is where data must be transformed into understanding and wisdom (see Chapter 5). Here is where data must be analyzed and triangulated (see Chapter 2).
8.	Select strategies for improvement	Strategies should be aimed at the identified cause(s) not at the symptoms. Strategies should be designed to dissolve the causes, not paper them over.
9.	Action plan	Develop an action plan to implement the strategies. Make sure to assign responsibilities, resources and timeline.

10.	Monitor and evaluate	Monitoring = are we doing what we said we would (action plan). If not, why not? Evaluation = is it making a difference?

This model is based upon the Planning Template provided in Preuss, P., (2002) *School Leader's Guide to Root Cause Analysis: Using Data to Dissolve Problems,* published by Eye On Education, Larchmont, NY.

Let's take a look at an example. This one involves a small centralized school district that has poor math achievement scores across the district as measured by recent state assessments. A K-12 "Math Committee" was convened by the Superintendent and a consultant was brought in to facilitate the group's work.

1.	What is the issue at hand?	Student proficiency in mathematics is insufficient across all grade levels.
2.	What is the ideal condition?	100% of all students achieving proficiency in mathematics at all grade levels.
3.	What is the present condition?	Less than 50% of all students achieve proficiency at all grade levels.
4.	What is the gap?	The gap varies by grade level but ranges between 60% and 70%.
5.	Is this a priority issue?	Yes, as it has become a major concern.
6.	Develop an "ends focused" goal statement.	The goal is to increase the percent of students testing at a proficient level on state assessments from the present level to 100% over the course of the next three years.
7.	Search for root cause	Here is where databased decision making becomes crucial. Teachers identified the textbook as not being in conformance with the state standards or state assessments, which was true. But a benchmarking process showed that a similar school, using the same textbook had significantly higher results. A faculty created survey also indicated that little grouping was done and that almost all instruction was "whole class."

8.	Select strategies for improvement	Strategy 1: Train instructional staff in using the text book as a resource, not as the curriculum. Strategy 2: Train teachers to truly know the state standards and means of assessing them. Strategy 3: Train teachers to develop parallel instructional processes and parallel teacher-developed assessments. Strategy 4: Train teachers in the process of using differentiated instruction and small groups. Strategy 5: Develop and implement a supervisory plan whereby school administration is prepared to support and enable the four strategies above. Strategy 6: Provide resources, time, talent, and funding in support of all items above.
9.	Action plan	Assign time-lines, responsibilities, and resources for each of the six strategies.
10.	Monitor and evaluate	Regularly monitor implementation of the strategies and evaluate results on at least a monthly basis.

Let's look at a second issue. The faculty at a regional Board of Cooperative Educational Services (BOCES) indicated that they felt there were far too many disciplinary incidents during the course of the school day and that steps should be taken to reduce their frequency. Fortunately each incident was recorded on a separate disciplinary referral card that contained detail about the cause of the referral, who referred the student, what time of day the incident occurred, and the home school of the student. Let's follow the process below as it unfolded in a committee.

1.	What is the issue at hand?	Too many student disciplinary referrals.
2.	What is the ideal condition?	No metric has been established determining what the ideal condition would look like. Perhaps the true ideal is zero. A more realistic number, given the age and type (alternative and vocational school students who are predominantly male) of student, would probably be higher.
3.	What is the present condition?	Staff feels that there are far too many disciplinary referrals during the course of each day. No metric has been established as to what is "far too many."
4.	What is the gap?	In this case – just a counting of disciplinary referrals by day, by week, by student, and by sending school, program, and IEP, would probably serve to demonstrate the frequency and patterns.
5.	Is this a priority issue?	Yes, as it has become a major faculty concern.

6.	Develop an "ends focused" goal statement.	The goal is to reduce student disciplinary referrals to an acceptable level within the next semester. In addition, the metric of what would be considered an acceptable level will be established.
7.	Search for root cause	Here is where the disciplinary referral cards assume importance because they contain a wealth of information. They must be analyzed for kind and time of infraction, sending school, and referring staff member. If available, cards from previous years can be likewise analyzed to determine if the pattern of referrals has changed or if it has remained stable. Looking at a single year's data, it was determined that over one third of all disciplinary referrals occurred during the noon hour. These incidents could be classified into four major types: driving away from the school without permission, transporting fellow students away from school without permission, and either negative interaction with the noontime monitors or student–to-student altercations. Upon looking at who the students were who became involved in these referrals it was found that the majority were from just three of the twelve sending schools. Another issue appeared, and that was that the majority of referrals coming from classroom disciplinary events came from just a handful of staff. Many staff had few incidents and some had none. Classroom incidents appeared to be relatively evenly distributed among the 12 sending schools. It was found that the three sending schools with the highest number of incidents were also the three schools that did not send a morning "pick-up" bus. Therefore their students had to wait until the afternoon bus arrived—creating a period of about 60 minutes when they were forced to wait
8.	Select strategies for improvement	Strategy 1: Seek cooperation from the three schools in sending a morning "pick-up" bus.
		Strategy 2: If schools will not or cannot cooperate by sending an additional bus, see if buses of other schools that pass through these neighboring districts would be willing to transport and drop-off these students.
		Strategy 3: If above strategies fail, seek the development of supervised programs for all students who must wait an hour for transport home.

		Strategy 4: Develop and implement a supervisory plan for those staff that have a high incidence of student misconduct.
		Strategy 5: Develop an agreed upon goal for what would be a satisfactory level of student disciplinary incidents.
		Strategy 6: Provide resources, time, talent, and funding in support of all items above.
9.	Action plan	Assign timelines, responsibilities, and resources for each of the five strategies.
10.	Monitor and evaluate	Regularly monitor implementation of the strategies and evaluate results on at least a monthly basis. Report out data on disciplinary referrals on a weekly basis to all staff.

The prior example provides only one possible flow of activities related to the issue of the frequency of student disciplinary referrals. Depending upon the initial data, the whole process might follow a completely different course, or, given the same data but a different context, the strategies might be different.

Remember the definition of DBDM: "DBDM is a system of deeply rooted beliefs, actions, and processes that infuses organizational culture and regularly transforms data to wisdom for the purpose of making organizational decisions."

In addition to understanding the process of DBDM we need to understand what types of data should be looked at and how we should go about organizing that data both mentally and physically.

Dr. Victoria Bernhardt is not only a prolific writer but an agile consultant, facilitator, and speaker as well. We first met when I served as manager for the New York Comprehensive Planning Technical Assistance Center and co-chaired New York State's Comprehensive District Education Planning (CDEP) steering committee. One of our committee members heard Dr. Bernhardt speak at a national convention and realized the need to bring her to New York in support of our efforts to spread the word about the use of data in comprehensive district planning. In fact, she had already written the book on a very similar process to our own (*The School Portfolio: A Comprehensive Framework for School Improvement*, 1994) Since that time she has returned to New York many times over and has been a force for positive change throughout the state.

Perhaps the most important initial concept that Dr. Bernhardt brought to us was the concept she called "multiple measures of data." It instantly gave us the ability to organize the "data swamp" and make it both manageable and serviceable. It was upon this framework, diagramed in Figure 2.1below, that our initial work with data in school districts was developed.

Figure 2.1. Dr. Victoria Bernhardt's Multiple Measures of Data

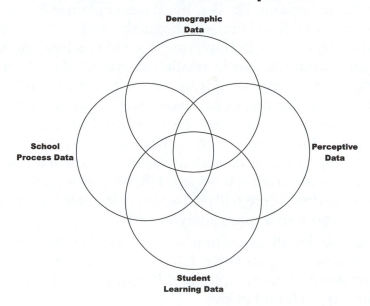

As can be seen, there are four major types of data: demographic data, perceptive data, student learning data, and school process data. Each of these areas of data is represented by a circle that intersects with each of the other three data areas. This separation of data into four discrete classifications was of immediate help in slogging our way through the data swamp. However the model goes into much greater detail as can be seen in Figure 2.2 below.

Figure 2.2. Multiple Measures of Data Expanded

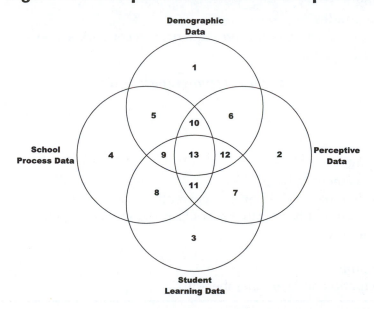

Each of these 13 cells has its own attributes and its own unique ability to provide insights into our system. Dr. Bernhardt has explained her model in great detail in each of her texts listed in the bibliography and I will not attempt to explain it in further detail here. In converting data to wisdom one has to look at multiple disaggregated data sets in relation to one another. That is what this model illustrates. Cell 13, for example, is the heart of the model where all four types of data converge. Dr. Bernhardt states that Cell 13 "allows the prediction of actions/processes/programs that best meet the learning needs of all students." The power of this model is significant when used in the hands of schools committed to the improvement of student learning. None of the four basic measures should be missing from a thorough DBDM process and the analysis of data should be relentless. More will be discussed about this necessity when we speak specifically about root cause analysis.

As mentioned above, all school data can be placed in one of four categories. It must be understood that qualitative data, such as perceptions, are equally important as quantitative data. Samples of different kinds of data and how they might be organized are found below.

Student Learning Data

Formative teacher-made assessments
Standardized assessment
Proficiency levels
Progress levels (see Chapter 3 on Value-Added Analysis)
Benchmarking of student achievement against self and other standards
Ability to perform in the workplace or college
"Kid Watching"
Teacher given grades*
Accumulation of course credits and sequences (secondary schools)*
College entrance exams

Student Demographic Data

Age
Gender
Ethnicity
Cohort grouping
Ability/Achievement to date
Programs student has been in or is in currently
Where has the student been (other schools, previous classes, etc.)
Socioeconomic level
Grade level
Location of home
School participation and/or "membership"

School System Processes

Retention rates
Attendance rates
Truancy rates
Identification rates and locations
Graduation rates
Dropout rates
Disciplinary rates
Time on task
Class cutting rates (secondary)
College acceptance rates and locations

Perceptive Data*

From students (before and after graduation)
From parents
From teachers and staff
From employers and other citizens
From college recruiters

Perceptions about what?

Satisfaction with student learning
Positive feelings of inclusion about school, staff & fellow students
Negative perceptions – things to be improved
Feelings about safety and discipline
Fairness
Ability to be heard, to have influence

I have marked three items in the outline above with an asterisk as an indicator that I want to focus on them in some detail here. The first item, "teacher given grades," is, in my experience, one of the more underrated data sets and yet I think it provides an accessible, frequent, and easily viewed window into the workings of the school. The most immediate purpose of providing students with grades, typically on a quarterly basis, is to provide students, parents, and teachers with feedback about student proficiency in the subject under study. Grades collectively, however, also communicate schoolwide patterns, patterns within and between departments and among teachers. They introduce questions such as:

♦ What is the failure rate? Where are the failures? Which departments, which classes, and which students have the higher rates of failure.

♦ Why do students fail? What is the major cause of failure?

♦ How can we eliminate failures while increasing standards?

♦ How does the school's system of grading compare to the school's standardized testing?

♦ Is there a correlation between assessment scores and teacher-given grades? If not, why not?

♦ Shouldn't our grading system communicate to student, parent, and teacher the same standard of proficiency as the state assessment program?

♦ Is there a correlation between grade levels in the grading process?

♦ As students move from grade level to grade level does the pattern of teacher-given grades change?

♦ What constitutes a grade: Is it homework; mastery of content; attendance?

Suffice it to say that the grading system is a storehouse of data waiting to be tapped in the pursuit of system wisdom.

The second area I marked is the "permanent record card." That is where one typically finds the number of credits and course sequences that students have earned during their secondary years. As high school principal I vividly remember the stack of permanent record cards that sat atop a filing cabinet in the guidance office following the graduation of each class. The stack would appear sometime in July and by the end of August it had disappeared, never to be seen again as a cohort group. In July, the individual cards were extracted from the folders of the recently graduated seniors and by the end of August they were alphabetically refilled among all of the school's previous graduates. The data on these cards, however, provide another wide window into the operation of the school as a learning system if one had the means and desire to look.

♦ How many units of credit had the school awarded? Where and to which students?

♦ How many failures did this class amass?

♦ How many students dropped-out before graduation? What was the cause?

♦ How many seniors did not graduate? What was the cause?

♦ How many course sequences were awarded and to which students?

♦ How many students had been given credit for multiple sequences and who were they?

♦ How many college credits were awarded to this class and to which students?

- ♦ How did the data from this class compare to the data from previous classes.

- ♦ Are any of the data sets considered to be key indicators of school success?

Once again the various data sets contained on these permanent record cards are crucial to gaining wisdom regarding the school's system.

The third area marked was that of Dr. Bernhardt's measure of "perceptive data." I think less of this kind of measure is gathered and used because it is time consuming, not already in place, and it takes a good deal of thought to develop instruments that adequately gather perceptive data. And yet its impact, like the others above, can be powerful. Perception gathering tools may range from a simple five-question survey of staff to a fifty- or hundred-question commercially prepared and tested annual survey of staff, parents, and students. One school district I worked with focused on the issue of student engagement in the school. They were concerned with the potential of isolated students who needed help and they wanted a general feel for how the student body viewed their school experience. It took a year to identify a commercially viable assessment tool and then the assessment was given near the end of each of the two school years before my departure from the system. What was of particular interest to me was that the responses from each of the two administrations of the survey were so similar. It gave me a feeling that we had indeed captured student perceptions of the school as seen through student responses to the perception survey.

Dr. Bernhardt is director of Education for the Future (EFF), a not-for-profit initiative located on the California State University Chico campus that focuses on working with schools, districts, State Departments of Education, and other educational service centers and agencies on systemic change and comprehensive data analyses that lead to increased student learning. The website: http://eff.csuchico.edu/home/Education for the Future provides free downloads of a series of questionnaires that have been used by them for some time. They also provide contracted services for use of the surveys and data analysis. Their website is a great resource for those interested in the development and use of questionnaires to gather perceptions.

I was contacted by a school district that was identified by its state education department as a school district in need of improvement. It was a small K-12 district with all students contained on the same campus. The district had already agreed with the suggestion of the state agency working with them to make use of the perception assessments provided by EFF and the district wanted me to both guide the administration of the surveys and to conduct the data analysis. The surveys not only contained fifty-three questions with multiple responses, but also provided space for individual responses to three open-ended questions

(What do I like about this school? What do I wish was different about this school? What do I wish you had asked about this school?). Surveys were completed by parents, students, and staff. Again, like so many other instances, as a consultant, I did not remain long enough to see the specific end results. The superintendent in this district, however, was a well-seasoned professional who had come out of retirement to serve as an interim superintendent to see this process through to its completion. I would like to share one of the student surveys as an example of how perceptive data can be used. I focus just on the student's responses to the 53–question survey and not their responses to the open-ended questions; although their open-ended responses were very illuminating—132 responses to the first question, 132 responses to the second, and 77 responses to third. Student responses were also serious—the manner in which the surveys were administered and the situation that the district was in somehow translated for the students that their perceptions mattered and would be used to improve their school.

Figure 2.3 provides the complete data set for the student survey. The 53 items are identified in the left hand columns while the average score (on a 1–5 scale) for each of the 5 grades are located in the central columns. On the scale, 1 was most negative and 5 was the most positive. The range among the 5 grade scores is listed in the column to the far right.

Figure 2.3. Education for the Future: High School Student Survey

Education for the Future - HS Student Survey

Ques	Page 1	Aver	8th	9th	10th	11th	12th	Range
	Grade Aver =		3.33	3.24	3.18	3.33	3.34	
	n =		15	51	18	19	22	
1a	I feel safe at this school	3.7	3.8	3.4	4.0	4.0	3.7	0.6
1b	I feel like I belong at this school	3.4	3.5	3.6	3.1	3.3	3.5	0.5
1c	I feel challenged at this school	2.8 *	2.8	2.8	2.8	2.7	2.8	0.1
1d	I have opportunities to choose my own projects	2.8 *	2.6	2.9	2.9	2.8	2.7	0.3
1e	I feel that I am in charge of what I learn	2.7	2.7	2.7	2.7	3.1	2.7	0.4
1f	Teachers encourage me to assess the quality of my own work	3.3	3.0	3.2	3.4	3.6	3.4	0.6
1g	This school is preparing me well for what I want to do after high school	2.7	3.3	2.8	2.6	2.6	2.1	1.2
1h	My teachers treat me fairly	3.1	3.0	2.9	3.0	3.5	3.5	0.6
1i	My school administrators treat me fairly	3.0	2.7	3.2	3.1	3.3	2.7	0.6
1j	My campus supervisors treat me fairly	3.1	3.3	3.2	3.1	3.4	3.0	0.4
1k	The office staff treat me fairly	3.2	3.0	3.3	2.9	3.4	3.2	0.5
1l	Other students at this school treat me fairly	3.6	3.3	3.4	3.5	3.8	3.9	0.6
1m	The work at this school is challenging	3.0	3.1	3.2	3.2	2.8	2.7	0.5
1n	I find what I learn in school to be relevant to real life	2.8	3.1	2.9	2.3	2.9	2.5	0.8
1o	I feel successful at school	3.2	3.3	3.1	3.0	3.4	3.4	0.4
1p	This school is fun	2.4 *	2.7	2.6	1.9	2.6	2.2	0.8
1q	I like this school	2.8	3.1	2.9	2.6	2.9	2.5	0.6
1r	I think this is a good school	2.8	3.1	2.8	2.8	2.9	2.5	0.6
1s	I like the students at this school	3.3	3.1	3.5	3.4	3.4	3.0	0.5
1t	Students at this school like me	3.7	3.5	3.6	3.7	3.7	3.7	0.2
1u	I like to learn	3.3	3.4	3.1	3.1	3.5	3.9	0.8
1v	Doing well in school makes me feel good about myself	3.8	3.7	3.7	3.6	3.6	4.1	0.5
1w	I am doing my best in school	3.7	3.8	3.8	3.8	3.4	3.8	0.4
1x	Participating in extracurricular activities is important to me	3.9	4.3	3.7	3.6	4.1	3.7	0.7

Figure 2.3. continues

		Aver		8th	9th	10th	11th	12th	
	My teachers:								
2a	expect students to do their best	3.9		4.2	3.8	3.9	3.8	4.1	0.4
2b	expect me to do my best	4.0		3.9	3.9	4.0	3.9	4.1	0.2
2c	are understanding when students have personal problems	2.8		2.6	2.8	2.8	3.0	3.1	0.5
2d	set high standards for learning in their classes	3.5		3.6	3.5	3.3	3.3	3.7	0.4
2e	help me gain confidence in my ability to learn	3.0		3.1	2.9	2.7	3.1	3.2	0.5
2f	know me well	3.2		3.6	3.0	3.0	3.1	3.5	0.6
2g	listen to my ideas	2.8		2.7	2.7	2.8	2.8	3.3	0.6
2h	care about me	2.9		2.7	2.8	2.6	3.1	3.4	0.8
2i	make learning fun	2.6	*	2.7	2.5	2.4	2.7	2.6	0.3
2j	are excited about the subject they teach	3.2		3.4	3.2	3.0	3.2	3.2	0.4
2k	give me individual attention when I need it	3.1		2.8	3.0	3.2	3.2	3.3	0.5
	I feel ready for the real world, with reference to:								
3a	my ability to write	3.7		3.7	3.8	3.5	3.4	3.6	0.4
3b	my ability to read	4.1		4.4	4.0	3.9	4.1	4.1	0.5
3c	my ability with mathematics	3.6		3.6	3.6	3.9	3.6	4.0	0.4
3d	my ability to process information	3.8		4.1	3.6	3.6	3.9	4.2	0.6
3e	my presentation skills	3.4		3.5	3.5	3.2	3.1	3.5	0.4
3f	my technology skills	3.7		4.1	3.6	3.8	3.3	4.2	0.9
3g	my ability to learn on my own outside of a classroom	4.1	*	4.3	4.0	4.0	4.1	4.4	0.4
	In my classes, my time is spent:								
4a	listening to the teacher talk	3.7		3.7	3.6	3.5	3.9	3.8	0.4
4b	in whole class discussions	3.0		3.0	3.2	2.8	2.8	2.8	0.4
4c	working in small groups	2.9		3.1	2.7	3.1	2.9	2.8	0.4
4d	answering questions from a book or worksheet	3.7		3.9	3.8	3.6	3.5	3.5	0.4
4e	working on projects or research	3.0		3.2	3.0	3.1	2.5	3.2	0.7
4f	doing work that I find meaningful	2.6		2.5	2.7	2.6	2.7	2.4	0.3
4g	using computers	2.7		3.1	2.7	2.8	2.3	2.9	0.8
	I learn well when:								
5a	I am working on projects or research	3.3		3.5	3.3	2.8	3.8	2.8	1.0
5b	the teacher is leading a discussion with the whole class	3.2		2.9	3.1	2.8	3.8	3.4	1.0
5c	I am working in a small group	3.6		3.7	3.7	3.3	3.7	3.5	0.4
5d	I am working by myself	3.5		3.1	3.6	3.3	3.6	3.7	0.6

Figure 2.4 provides a simplified graph of the data in Figure 2.3 by using the range of average scores for each grade level. The benefit is that we have a simple graph covering a lot of data. The detriment is that we lose a lot of information by using averages and a range. But in any event, Figure 2.4 is sufficient for my purpose at this point in explaining the importance and use of perceptive data.

When I first printed out a more complex line chart of the student responses to the 53 questions from the five different grade levels I was more than surprised to see how the data from the 5 grades "danced" with each other. Perhaps most people can easily see that same relationship by scanning the data table in Figure 2.3 however as a visual learner it helps me to better understand by seeing data graphically.

Figure 2.4 presents the range of item response averages by grade level for each of the 53 survey items. Item 1a, for example, has a range of 0.6, from a low response average of 3.4 in ninth grade to a high response average of 4.0 in both the tenth and eleventh grades. By glancing at the graph one can see visually that there is a certain degree of "tightness" to each of the ranges. Using item 1a as our example once again, it has a range of 0.6, which appears to be among the most frequent sized ranges, but if one refers to Figure 2.3 you can see that if the ninth-grade average was not considered, the range would be reduced to 0.3. My point, as I mentioned above, is that a lot of information has been lost in creating a simplified graphic. However, the simplified graphic helps to more easily illustrate the choreography of the average student responses across the 1 to 5 range. As the consultant working with this school district, the close choreography among and between the 5 different grade levels, amplified by their written responses to the 3 open-ended questions, led me to believe that the students were both sincere in their responses to the survey and in their willingness to help the district in what everyone recognized as difficult times. Furthermore, their responses appeared to me to be more uniform and harmonious with each other than fractured and discordant. Students appeared to be speaking from a similar point of view no matter their grade level. In brief, these student perceptions were of great value and needed to be considered as part of the data resources being considered in the development of the school's improvement planning process.

Figure 2.4. Education for the Future: High School Student Survey Range of Item Response Averages by Grade Level

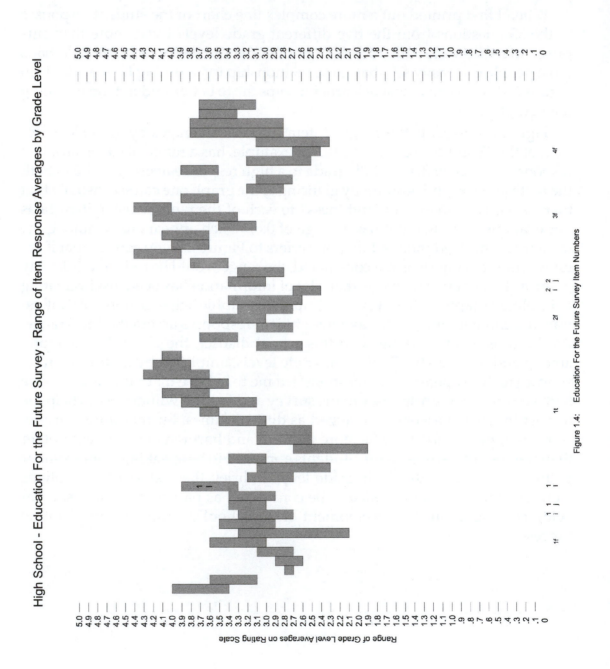

Figure 2.5 simply tabulates the distribution of ranges among the 53 items. Out of curiosity I would look at those largest ranges, items 1g, 5a, and 5b to try to discover why such large differences occurred. In each case it appears to be the function of wide differences among just 2 grade levels. Thirty-one items have a range of 0.5 or less and of these sixteen have a range of only 0.4.

Figure 2.5 Distribution of Ranges

Range	Number of Items
0.1	1
0.2	2
0.3	3
0.4	16
0.5	9
0.6	11
0.7	2
0.8	5
0.9	1
1.0	2
1.1	0
1.2	1

The combined data from all secondary grade levels is presented in Figure 2.6. There is a lot of information to consider on these two pages. First, let me review the data format. The item identifiers are listed in the left column. The actual item prompt is then listed to the right of the identifier. The average of all student responses for each item is then listed. The total number of students responding to each item on the 1 to 5 scale is then posted. The sum of the students responding with either a 1 or 2 is totaled as is the sum of students responding with either a 4 or 5. In the final column on the far right side the difference between those responding 1 or 2 (negatively) and 4 or 5 (positively) is listed. In addition, the mode (greatest number of responses) is identified by printing the number in bold.

Figure 2.6. Education for the Future HS Student Survey: Negative and Positive Responses

Ques	Pg 1	Aver	1	2	3	4	5	Sum 1&2	Sum 4&5	Diff.
1a	I feel safe at this school	3.7	4	6	35	67	17	10	84	74
1b	I feel like I belong at this school	3.4	9	17	33	49	21	26	70	44
1c	I feel challenged at this school	2.8	17	28	56	23	5	45	28	-17
1d	I have opportunities to choose my own projects	2.8	17	34	39	37	2	51	39	-12
1e	I feel that I am in charge of what I learn	2.7	24	29	39	30	7	53	37	-16
1f	Teachers encourage me to assess the quality of my own work	3.3	10	15	38	54	11	25	65	40
1g	This school is preparing me well for what I want to do after high school	2.7	28	28	40	25	8	56	33	-23
1h	My teachers treat me fairly	3.1	16	20	35	44	13	36	57	21
1i	My school administrators treat me fairly	3.0	19	17	42	42	9	36	51	15
1j	My campus supervisors treat me fairly	3.1	12	14	52	45	6	26	51	25
1k	The office staff treat me fairly	3.2	12	20	40	46	11	32	57	25
1l	Other students at this school treat me fairly	3.6	12	13	19	55	29	25	84	59
1m	The work at this school is challenging	3.0	12	20	57	31	9	32	40	8
1n	I find what I learn in school to be relevant to real life	2.8	22	26	42	34	4	48	38	-10
1o	I feel successful at school	3.2	12	18	43	44	12	30	56	26
1p	This school is fun	2.4	36	29	40	21	2	65	23	-42
1q	I like this school	2.8	29	15	45	26	13	44	39	-5
1r	I think this is a good school	2.8	23	26	37	32	10	49	42	-7
1s	I like the students at this school	3.3	10	15	39	43	19	25	62	37
1t	Students at this school like me	3.7	5	11	28	64	21	16	85	69
1u	I like to learn	3.3	17	10	39	46	17	27	63	36
1v	Doing well in school makes me feel good about myself	3.8	9	6	25	55	34	15	89	74
1w	I am doing my best in school	3.7	4	13	30	49	33	17	82	65
1x	Participating in extracurricular activities is important to me	3.9	7	10	28	33	51	17	84	67

Figure 2.6. continues

		Aver	1	2	3	4	5	Sum 1&2	Sum 4&5	Diff.
My teachers:										
2a	expect students to do their best	3.9	1	6	21	73	28	7	101	94
2b	expect me to do my best	4.0	2	3	22	74	28	5	102	97
2c	are understanding when students have personal problems	2.8	20	25	49	25	10	45	35	-10
2d	set high standards for learning in their classes	3.5	2	9	52	51	14	11	65	54
2e	help me gain confidence in my ability to learn	3.0	10	31	48	32	8	41	40	-1
2f	know me well	3.2	18	16	38	41	16	34	57	23
2g	listen to my ideas	2.8	19	23	50	33	4	42	37	-5
2h	care about me	2.9	21	14	58	29	7	35	36	1
2i	make learning fun	2.6	24	31	55	17	2	55	19	-36
2j	are excited about the subject they teach	3.2	9	21	50	36	13	30	49	19
2k	give me individual attention when I need it	3.1	16	18	46	35	14	34	49	15
I feel ready for the real world, with reference to:										
3a	my ability to write	3.7	7	9	30	54	29	16	83	67
3b	my ability to read	4.1	2	5	20	62	42	5	104	99
3c	my ability with mathematics	3.6	11	6	33	51	29	16	80	64
3d	my ability to process information	3.8	2	6	29	64	27	8	91	83
3e	my presentation skills	3.4	8	17	43	40	21	25	61	36
3f	my technology skills	3.7	5	8	39	45	32	13	77	64
3g	my ability to learn on my own outside of a classroom	4.1	1	3	21	62	42	4	104	100
In my classes, my time is spent:										
4a	listening to the teacher talk	3.7	4	7	35	63	20	11	83	72
4b	in whole class discussions	3.0	5	36	52	29	7	41	36	-5
4c	working in small groups	2.9	10	30	53	30	5	40	25	-15
4d	answering questions from a book or worksheet	3.7	1	9	37	65	17	10	82	72
4e	working on projects or research	3.0	8	29	56	28	8	37	36	-1
4f	doing work that I find meaningful	2.6	27	24	49	23	5	51	28	-23
4g	using computers	2.7	15	38	50	18	8	53	26	-27
I learn well when:										
5a	I am working on projects or research	3.3	13	21	33	42	20	34	62	28
5b	the teacher is leading a discussion with the whole class	3.2	13	20	41	36	19	33	55	22
5c	I am working in a small group	3.6	6	11	36	51	25	17	76	59
5d	I am working by myself	3.5	11	12	32	49	25	23	74	51

My first facilitating question working with groups seeking root cause is "What do you see in this data set?" There are a lot of things to be seen in this data and it would be wise to hand this out at least several days before the facilitation session. Let me identify several items that I "see."

Item 1p: "This school is fun" is the lowest rated item on the page. This is reinforced on page 2 by Item 2i: "My teachers make learning fun." Again the lowest rated item on the page. Notice also the relative weighting on the negative side of the scoring "see/saw." Item 1p has a difference of -42 and item 2i has a difference of -36. Both are substantially lower than any other difference scores. It seems that the students are telling us something.

There is also a sense that students do not feel in control or do not feel as active participant in the structure of their learning. This is shown by messages that students sent in responses to items listed in Figure 2.7.

Figure 2.7. Student Messages Regarding Control

		Average	*Sum 1&2*	*Sum 3&4*
Item 1c:	"I feel challenged at this school."	2.8	45	28
Item 1d:	"I have opportunities to choose my own projects."	2.8	51	39
Item 1e:	"I feel that I am charge of what I learn."	2.7	53	37
Item 2c:	"My teachers are understanding"	2.8	45	35
Item 2g:	"My teachers listen to my ideas."	2.8	42	37
Item 2h:	"My teachers care about me."	2.9	35	36
Item 4c:	"My time is spent working in small groups."	2.9	40	35
Item 5c:	"I learn well when I work in small groups."	3.6	17	76
Item 4f:	"My time is spent doing work that I find meaningful."	2.6	51	28

In Section 3 the students provide nearly all positive responses to items about their readiness for the real world—the strongest showing is on "my ability to learn on my own outside of a classroom" (3g) and "my ability to read" (3a)—both scored at an average of 4.1 out of 5. And yet, item 1g, "this school is preparing me well for what I want to do after high school" is rated at only a 2.7.

These are just some of the things I see in this data. Of course, as a facilitator I would never share these observations; the group has to "see" with their own eyes and hence my first question of them would be, as indicated above, "What do you see in this data?" Because of the complexity of the data set it would be absolutely necessary to hand it out several days before but not too soon lest it becomes forgotten.

The next question in the facilitation process of converting data into information, into knowledge, into understanding, and into wisdom is, and in seeking root cause, is: "What questions do you have about what you see?" If for example, the issue of student learning styles and preferences against what appears to be the instructional style of the school came up, perhaps it would be wise to explore the difference between the answers given in Section 3 and to that given to item 1g ("this school is preparing me well for what I want to do after high school"). The issues of teacher listening, caring about, and understanding their students might also prove to be fertile areas of exploration. Maybe the teachers do listen and care, but it is not being perceived by the students to the degree that I am sure the staff would want.

Because these surveys were anonymous it was not possible to cross reference answers to other data such as grade point average, attendance, special programs, etc. We did gather certain self-reported demographic data regarding: ethnicity, grade level, gender, graduation plans, and extra curricular participation that we used to compare disaggregated groups. It would be nice, however, if someone developed an anonymous process that enabled these other cross references.

I also computed what I considered to be a "student satisfaction score." This score was based on each individual's average (mean) response to items 1a through 3g. This *student satisfaction score* was used to compare various demographic groupings of students which are reported on in Figure 2.8 below. The mean for all student satisfaction scores was 3.27.

Figure 2.8. Student Satisfaction Scores by Demographic Factors

Group	n	Satisfaction Score
Male	67	3.22
Female	62	3.33
College Bound	79	3.34
Other Plans	50	3.16
Participants in after school activities	104	3.33
Nonparticipants	25	3.02
Athletics only	40	3.26
One or two activities	87	3.31
Three or more activities	17	3.47

Few of the differences above are remarkable and many appeal to our stereotypes.

The distribution of student satisfaction scores formed a continuum from a low of 1.55 to a high of 4.60 (all students all grade levels). Again this was visual confirmation that the students were not broken into separate modalities of satisfaction but rather constituted a continuum of degrees of satisfaction. I would venture to say, however, that the student scoring 1.55 and the student scoring 4.6 attend entirely different schools and that these satisfaction scores are based upon their own perceptions and perhaps a certain degree of reality. In order to explore these extremes further I took a look at the item ratings for the 13 students with the highest mean satisfaction score (ranging from 3.90 to 4.60) and for the 17 students with the lowest mean satisfaction score (ranging from an individual mean score of 1.55 to 2.64) and then looked at the items with the greatest discrepancy (-2.5 pts or higher). These items are listed below in Figure 2.9, indicating the item identifier, discrepancy, and item narrative. The numbers in parenthesis indicate the mean of the high and low scoring groups.

Figure 2.9. Major Discrepancy Listing: High- and Low-Satisfaction Scoring Students

Item		Item narrative
1b	-2.8	I feel like I belong in this school (4.6/1.8)
1g	-2.5	This school is preparing me well for what I want to do after high school. (4.0/1.5)
1h	-2.8	My teachers treat me fairly. (4.5/1.7)
1i	-2.7	My administrators treat me fairly. (4.3/1.6)
1k	-2.5	The office staff treat me fairly. (4.5/2.0)
1q	-3.0	I like this school. (4.2/1.2)
1r	-2.9	I think this is a good school. (4.1/1.2)

Forgive me, but as a former high school principal I almost immediately conjure up a stereotypical image of who these students are, what they look like and how they behave. Yet these are the very students that need to arrive at the point of proficiency before graduation if not long before. How many years have these students harbored these feelings about the people and place where they spend most of their daylight hours? Can we trace it back upstream? Is it a function of poor grades (proficiency) leading to poor discipline leading to high absence? Is it a function of slow progress dragging the student forever further and further behind? What are the dynamic causal factors? Can we change them? How many of the ninth graders in the low group will ever achieve a diploma? Indeed, how many of all 17 will graduate with a diploma?

A partial demographic breakdown of both the 17 low-satisfaction students and 13 high-satisfaction students is presented below in Figure 2.10

Figure 2.10. Demographic Features of High- and Low-Satisfaction Students

	Low Group	High Group
Male	10	6
Female	7	7
Grade 8	1	3
Grade 9	8	6
Grade 10	1	0
Grade 11	3	3
Grade 12	2	2
No extra curricular activity	8	0
Involved in athletics	7	10
Involved in more than one activity	3	9

There were also areas where students in both groups nearly converged in their rating of an item. I used a measure of 1.0 or less as the determinant factor. The items, discrepancy, and item narrative are shown below in Figure 2.11. Again the numbers in parenthesis indicate the mean scores of the high and low groups.

Figure 2.11. Major Convergent Listing: High- and Low-Satisfaction–Scoring Students

Item		Item narrative
1l	-1.0	Other students at this school treat me fairly. (4.3/3.3)
1m	-1.0	The work at this school is challenging. (3.4/2.4)
3f	-1.0	I feel ready for the real world, with reference to my technology skills. (4.3/3.3)
3g	-0.8	I feel ready for the real world, with reference to my ability to learn on my own outside of a classroom. (4.5/3.7)

Interestingly a number of near convergent score points between the low- and high-satisfaction groups occurred in the nonsatisfaction items found in sections 4 and 5 of the survey. Again, the numbers in parenthesis indicate the mean score of the high and low groups. These items are listed below in Figure 2.12.

Figure 2.12. Major Convergent Listing: High- and Low-Satisfaction– Scoring Students in *Nonsatisfaction* Items

Item		*Item narrative*
4a	-0.7	In my classes, my time is spent listening to the teacher talk. (3.8/3.1)
4c	-0.3	In my classes my time is spent in working in small groups. (3.1/2.8)
4d	-0.5	In my classes my time is spent answering questions from a book or worksheet. (3.9/3.4)
4e	-0.6	In my classes my time is spent on projects or research. (3.5/2.9)
4g	-0.3	In my classes my time is spent using computers. (2.8/2.5)
5d	-0.9	I learn well when working by myself. (3.5/2.6)

One might hypothesize, based on these reported perceptions, that the instructional experiences of these two groups of students are somewhat similar. This is what I see in this data set and I would have to develop my questions about what I see to guide further investigation of the hypothesis.

The difference between male and female students was slight. The mean male satisfaction score was 3.21 and the female mean was 3.34. The Pearson's Correlation is 0.874 between the two sets of item responses.

Teachers were also asked to complete a survey. In fact they completed two identical surveys. The first was of their perceptions; the second was their prediction of what student perceptions would be. Although teachers predicted that the students would be more negative in their response to all items (satisfaction score of 2.89) students responded with a more positive perception (satisfaction score of 3.27). In fact student response to all items was generally positive as can be seen in Figure 2.13 below.

**Figure 2.13. Frequency and Percentage
of Student Responses (1 to 5)**

Response (1–5)	Frequency	Percent
1	657	8.0%
2	925	11.3%
3	2099	25.6%
4	2253	27.5%
5	2253	27.4%

After scoring the surveys, tabulating the results, and reading their responses to the open-ended questions I came away with the very strong sense that the students were telling it as they saw it in an honest attempt to help the system improve, or perhaps in the case of the low-satisfaction students, to indict the system for its failing them.

The state education department had also conducted surveys of staff and parents that became part of this project. Working through the parent-teacher organization parents were surveyed with the EFF instrument. Younger students were queried using age-appropriate surveys with smiley faces. There was a mass of perceptive data that provided a large window into the system from a variety of vantage points.

In some ways this process proceeded from the concept of casting a wide net of survey questions in order to see what was caught. One could then decide if what was caught had any bearing on the issue at hand: – the need for the school district to improve student learning outcomes at all levels. Without firm guidance and discipline it would become easy for the process to meander off into an interesting but perhaps useless digression. The necessary guidance and discipline should come from those leading the project as well as a focus upon the key indicators of student and district success. The concept of key indicators is covered in Chapter 5. Hopefully my point is made that perceptive data can provide a wide window into the system and must be included in DBDM so that as complete a picture as possible is available for study.

Before concluding this chapter, I must make the point that successful DBDM ultimately requires the support of a robust data-rich infrastructure. The development of such an infrastructure begins with the active and visible support by the district's leadership through the:

♦ allocation and gathering of necessary resources;

♦ modeling of their use; and

♦ expectation of their use by staff in problem solving.

Successful DBDM also enables a smooth transition to Dynamic Planning that is covered in Chapter 6. In Chapter 7, *Making It Happen*, addresses in further detail, the issues associated with developing the necessary data infrastructure.

Summary

In this chapter considerable space was dedicated to looking at how numerous others define, explain, or make use of DBDM. Additional Resources, at the end of this chapter, provides the website addresses recommended for further study into DBDM. Our own definition of DBDM has been presented as well as models that offer specific examples of its use. We have very briefly presented Dr. Victoria Bernhardt's concept of "Multiple Measures of Data" as a means of clarifying the four types of data that must be used in combination in any DBDM process. Considerable space has been taken in exploring the potential and use of perceptive data using as an example the results from one survey process in which surveys from Education for the Future (EFF) were used. The importance of developing a robust data infrastructure was identified and it was pointed out that successful DBDM processes enable a smooth transition to Dynamic Planning, which is the subject of Chapter 6. It is hoped that this chapter has provided the groundwork for and encourages readers to identify how DBDM can be used within their own system.

Questions to Think About

1. At what "stage" is my system in the development and use of DBDM?
    - ☐ Haven't started yet
    - ☐ Beginning
    - ☐ Intermediate
    - ☐ Advanced
2. If my system is less than "advanced," what is needed to move to the next "stage"?
3. Try using Force Field Analysis to assist in identifying driving and restraining forces.
4. As an individual, how comfortable am I in using data in making decisions?
    - ☐ Not at all comfortable
    - ☐ Somewhat comfortable
    - ☐ Usually comfortable
    - ☐ Very Comfortable
5. If I am less than "very comfortable," what do I need to move to the next level?

Additional Resources

Fourteen additional Internet resources investigated in preparing this chapter are listed here. Those eager to conduct further research on this topic will find ample additional materials to study.

1. Data-driven decision making is the process of making choices based on appropriate analysis of relevant information. School district decision makers are using technology and professional expertise to improve instruction and operations. http://www.3d2know.org/

2. The National Education Technology Plan, *Toward A New Golden Age in American Education* calls upon states, districts, and schools to establish a plan to integrate data systems; use data from both administrative and instructional systems to understand relationships; ensure interoperability; and use assessment results to inform instruction. www.NationalEdTechPlan.org

    This same report provides a technology framework for No Child Left Behind success that includes the following ten components:

Data Systems:	getting the right data
Performance Standards:	getting the right data
Data Standards:	getting the data right
Data Quality:	getting the data right
Aligned Assessment Measures:	getting the data the right way
Automated Data Systems:	getting the data the right way
Data Consolidation, Security, and access:	getting the data the right way
Network Connectivity:	getting the data right away
Electronic Exchange of Records:	getting the data right away
Technology Infrastructure:	get the right data management

    The purpose of this technology framework is to break down the walls of isolated data sets by aggregation of data into large scale data warehouses, which can then be queried for the purpose of reporting out answers to specific questions, which, in turn, will inform the instructional decision-making process thereby enabling continuous school improvement.

3. Learning Point Associates (www.ncrel.org) (The North Central Regional Educational Lab) has a fine site with numerous resources for

the use of data in education, including a 28-page white paper that is free for the asking or may be downloaded quickly. The closest I could come to a finding a specific definition for data-driven decision making, however, is found in the description of the four part school improvement cycle (Plan, Do, Study, Act) found at the bottom of page 3 and reproduced here:

"Data are the key to continuous improvement. When you "plan" you must use data to provide insight and focus for your goals. Data patterns reveal strengths and weaknesses in the system and provide excellent direction. When you "do," you collect data that will tell you the impact of your strategies. Through collaborative reflection (explained earlier), you "study" the feedback offered by your data and begin to understand when to stay the course and when to make changes. Then you "act" to refine your strategies. Eventually the whole cycle begins again."

4. A six-page publication at Mid-continent Research for Education and Learning (McREL) ttp://www.mcrel.org/P_Hlt161047207DBM_7_F/LeadershipOrganizationDevelopment/5031TG_datafolio.pdf identified these key elements for data-driven decision making:

   ▪ Purposeful data collection & analysis
   ▪ Designated resources and other supports such as time and an appropriate data-management system
   ▪ Strategies for communicating about the process of data collection and use as well as the findings

   The same six-page publication contains a brief rubric covering each of the three key elements noted above and organized by these action descriptors: least effective, somewhat effective, and most effective.

5. The Middle States Commission of Secondary Education (*www.css-msa.org*) has at least two standards that directly address the issue of databased decision making without ever mentioning the term. The two standards are:

   Standard 11: Assessment of Student Learning: "The assessment of student learning outcomes enables students to monitor their own learning progress and allows teachers to adapt their instruction to the specific learning needs of students. The school's effectiveness is assessed by examining areas such as student learning and performance, program evaluation, performance results for support services, graduate success, and client satisfaction. Results are used to develop strategies for improving service and program quality. Assessment results are communicated appropriately to parents/ guardians, students, staff, and school community."

Standard 12: Planning: "The school makes use of strategic, long-range, and operational planning to continuously improve its educational programs and services. Improvement plans focus on student performance and organizational growth and engender continuous improvement across all aspects of the school organization. Externally validated processes for evaluation, strategic planning, and school/district improvement are continuously maintained. Systematic analysis regarding student performance and organizational growth is coupled with analysis of instructional and organizational practices to ensure alignment with the school's philosophy, mission, beliefs, and/or objectives. Trends in outcomes and results are projected and goals of demonstrated strategic merit are identified."

Each of the standards above is coupled with descriptions of numerous indicators.

6. Dr. Victoria Bernhardt's numerous texts contain a series of detailed rubrics that she calls "Continuous Improvement Continuums," which are suggested for use as "vehicles for ongoing self-evaluation." Three of these deal directly with the concept of data-driven decision making: the Information and Analysis Continuum; the Student Achievement Continuum; and the Quality Planning Continuum. Each continuum contains on its horizontal axis five levels of expectations starting with the lowest (1) and concluding with the highest (5). The vertical access contains the following three stages of development: Approach, Implementation and Outcome.

The level five outcomes for each of three continuums mentioned above are:

Information and Analysis: "Students are delighted with the school's instructional processes and proud of their own capabilities to learn and assess their own growth. Good to excellent achievement is the result for all students. No student falls through the cracks. Teachers use data to predict and prevent potential problems."

Student Achievement: "Students and teachers conduct self assessments to continuously improve performance. Improvements in student achievement are evident and clearly caused by teachers' and students' understanding of individual student learning standards, linked to appropriate and effective instructional and assessment strategies. A continuum of learning results. No students fall through the cracks."

Quality Planning: "Evidence of effective teaching and learning results in significant improvement of student achievement attributed to quality planning at all levels of the school organization. Teachers and administrators understand and share the school mission and vision. Quality planning is seamless and all demonstrate evidence of accountability."

Dr. Bernhardt maintains an extensive website at Education for the Future (*http://eff.csuchico.edu/home/*).

7. Many educators are aware of The Malcolm Baldridge National Quality Award for Schools (go to *www.quality.nist.gov*). The criteria and processes of evaluation for schools build upon previous criteria for businesses. An 88-page overview of the current process and educational criteria is available at the website listed above. Of the 7-criteria categories listed, category 4 is of the most interest to us at this moment. Category 4 is Measurement and Analysis, and contains two subsections: 4.1 Measurement, Analysis, and Improvement of Organizational performance, and 4.2 Management of Information, Information Technology, and Knowledge. Category 4 is worth 90 points out of a total of 1000. The only categories with a higher point value are leadership and results. The following is taken from page 4 of the 2007 Education Criteria for Performance Excellence:

"**Management by Fact:** Organizations depend upon the measurement and analysis of performance. Such measures should derive from the organization's needs and strategy, and they should provide critical data and information about key processes and results. Many types of data and information are needed for performance management. Performance measurement should focus on student learning, which requires a comprehensive and integrated fact-based system—one that includes input data, environmental data, performance data, comparative/competitive data, workforce data, cost data, and operational performance measurement. Measurement areas might include student's backgrounds, learning styles, aspirations, academic strengths and weaknesses, educational progress, classroom and program learning, satisfaction with instruction and services, extracurricular activities, dropout/matriculation rates and postgraduation success. Examples of appropriate data segmentation include segmentation by student learning results, student demographics, and workforce groups.

Analysis refers to extracting larger meaning from data and information to support evaluation, decision making, and improvement. Analysis entails using data to determine trends, projections, and cause and effect that might not otherwise be evident. Analysis supports a variety of purposes, such as planning, reviewing overall performance, improving operations, accomplishing change management, and comparing your performance with that of organizations providing similar programs and services or with best practices benchmarks."

8. The California Learning Resource Network defines Data-Driven Decision Making (DDDM) in the following way: "A DDDM focus uses student assessment data and relevant background information, to inform decisions related to planning and implementing instructional strategies at the district, school, classroom, and individual student levels." (http://www.clrn.org/elar/dddm.cfm#A)

9. The Council of Chief State School Officers has a very fine website "Databased Decision Making: Resources for Educators located at www.ael.org/dbdm. Interestingly, the site does not refer to either DBDM or D3M in its glossary. It does, however, provide a definition of sorts in its answer to "Why Use Data?":

"School improvement is the ultimate goal of school reform laws and the rules, policies, and procedures for implementing them. Federal and many state laws require schools to have school improvement plans and to set goals to improve student achievement of standards. Goals for improvement are based on state and local assessment results and the indicator systems of which they are a part. These results reveal overall learning, conditions that affect learning, and discrepancies in learning between content areas, groups of students, and grade levels. Using this information, the school determines what needs to be improved, who needs to improve, and how that improvement might be accomplished."

10. The Education Commission of the States has a fine four-page (2002) document entitled "Data-Driven Decision making" in their series of "No Child Left Behind Issue Briefs." The document is located at *http://www.ecs.org/clearinghouse/35/52/3552.pdf* and contains the sub-headings:

▪ Types of Data Districts Collect.

- Tracking Student Achievement for Diagnosis and Placement
- Changing Beliefs and Attitudes That All Children Can Learn
- Guiding Teachers' Professional Development
- Interventions and Curricular Decisions
- Using Data to Create School Improvement Plans and Assess Progress
- Allocating District Resources
- How Districts Use Data
- How Schools Support Data Use
- The Future of District Data Use.

11. The website of the Montgomery County Schools of Maryland contains significant information regarding their use of the Baldrige criteria to improve learning for students. Their brief Baldrige definition of "Management by Fact" is that it "occurs when data is used to drive decisions, inform instruction, and/or to evaluate key processes and results." Interestingly, for a district with such a fine website and so much information regarding their use of the Baldrige criteria, I found it almost impossible to locate the information from their home page. Fortunately they have a website search function that, when used, provides rapid access to their Baldrige pages. The webpage listed below contains descriptors for management by fact for schools, classes and students as well as links to many other pages containing information on the criteria for staff leadership, students and parents. (*http://www.mcps.k12.md.us/info/baldrige/about/values/fact.shtm#school*). In a review of over two hundred Google citations it appears that nearly all of the educational use of the term "Management by Facts" can be attributed to the Malcolm Baldrige process.

12. The Spring 2001 Newsletter of the Comprehensive Center – Region VI, located at the University of Wisconsin at Madison, is a 40 page document which focuses on "Using Data for Educational Decision-Making". This newsletter contains eleven articles on a wide variety of data related issues and In the introduction, processes. written by then Director, Walter G. Secada, the following expanded operational definition of DDDM is given:

"Increasingly, educators and interested policy makers use terms like "using data" and "data-driven decision making". In part, this new terminology reflects business models of decision making, such as total quality management, where data are collected and used in real time to monitor how well a particular process is working, to identify bottlenecks in a system, to make short-term plans, to engage in long-range strategic planning, to evaluate personnel performance, and other purposes. The salience given to data-driven decision making is also an acknowledgement that educators gather data that never are analyzed or used as fully as they might." *http://www.wcer.wisc.edu/ archive/ccvi/pub/newsletter/v6n1_Spr01.pdf*

13. The Washington State Technology Alliance has web pages devoted to elements of what they describe as the "paradigm shift to data-driven decision making" in schools. "The Technology Alliance is a statewide organization founded in 1996 to promote a vibrant technology-based economy benefiting Washington and its citizens. A CEO-level board comprised of leaders from business and research institutions directs the TA's work" Their web site is found at: *http://www.technology-alliance.com/pubspols/dddm/paradigmshift.html*. The only specific definition of DDDM is that contained on one of the PowerPoint slides as written by the NSSE in 1998. The following subtopics are also discussed, mainly in the form of citations from other publications:

- Top 10 uses of data in schools
- Attributes of districts that make wise use of data
- Making the case for data-driven decision making (+ 16 slide PowerPoint)
- Beginning the dialogue: A video-centered discussion
- Considerations for data analysis
- Types of data
- Considerations for the data collected
- Considerations for the disaggregation of data
- The inquiry cycle

14. In the state of Ohio the **D3A2 Project** (Data Driven Decisions for Academic Achievement) has been establish for the purposes listed below:

The D3A2 will be based upon a technical infrastructure that integrates and enhances existing systems to meet the following five objectives:

1. **D3A2 Content Exchange -** Provide educators with electronic access to education content resources aligned to Ohio's Academic Content Standards.

2. **D3A2 Local Data Analysis** - Provide access to a data warehouse and business intelligence tools for data analysis and decision

making at the local education agency level – including teacher access to individual student data.

3. **D3A2 State Required Reporting -** Provide an efficient and effective system for local education agencies to exchange data with ODE.

4. **D3A2 Statewide Longitudinal Data Analysis -** Provide a statewide longitudinal data warehouse for research, analysis, and decision making by a variety of stakeholders

5. **D3A2 Federal Required Data Reporting -** Provide an automated, streamlined process to support reporting of federally required data. *http://d3a2.org/status.asp*

3
Data Pathways

Some few years ago, while I was attending a quarterly meeting of the New York Schools Data Analysis Group (www.datag.org), I began to list all of the ways in which school data was being discussed and used. This list soon provided the basis for my development of a schematic that I have called "Data Pathways Leading to Root Cause." Figure 3.1 below presents the initial three layers of the schematic.

Figure 3.1. Data Pathways Leading to Root Cause

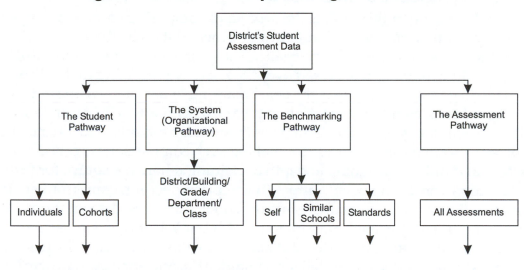

In this example, the top box is labeled "District's Student Assessment Data" as that is the type of data we are focusing on in this text. The concept of "data pathways," however, is appropriate for use with many other types of data such as: other student proficiency or progress data, student management data, and financial data. It should also be understood that the term "student assessment data," within the context of this text, means both assessment of proficiency (achievement) and assessment of progress (growth). Chapter 4 is focused on the concept of "value added analysis" that uses both proficiency and progress to measure instructional effectiveness.

The second layer contains the four data pathways in which student assessment data is being used and I believe that all uses of student data can be placed on one of these four pathways: Student Pathway, System Pathway,

Benchmarking Pathway, and the Assessment Pathway. I use the term pathway as a metaphor for the four possible investigative routes that should be taken in both converting data to information to knowledge to understanding to wisdom and in seeking root causes for both problems and successes.

The third layer breaks these four pathways into their component lanes. Again, the concept of lane is a metaphor for yet a smaller, finer, investigative process where data is examined at greater detail. The student pathway, for example, contains a lane for the analysis of individual student data as well as another lane for the analysis of cohort student data. There may be numerous cohorts being studied, such as gender, ethnicity, sending school or class, socioeconomic level, location of home, school groupings, and so on.

Likewise the system or organizational pathway contains lanes for buildings, grades, departments, programs, class groupings, and the district as a whole. The many lanes are shown in a single box for the purpose of simplification but some or all of these lanes are being used by school districts depending upon their need and sophistication in using student assessment data for both the analysis of progress and achievement.

Benchmarking in this case, is the process of comparing student assessment results with other measures of student assessment data. The three sources comprise the three lanes in this schematic. The first lane is the comparison, or benchmarking of data, against self over time. Are we changing in the direction we need to go? A second lane is the benchmarking of data against the data from similar schools. Similarity most often means a school that is of similar size, within a similar geographic setting, with similar students and financial resources. A sophisticated process for making such comparisons is called *frontier analysis* and rather than going in depth explaining it here the source for further information can be found at: http://www.prismdecision.com/frontier_analyst.cfm. Benchmarking against similar schools answers the question: How does our student learning compare to the student learning in similar schools? Frontier analysis also provides the answer to the question: Which similar schools are most effective in delivering student proficiency and growth? The third benchmarking lane is the comparison of student assessment data against local, state, and national standards. How proficient are our students in comparison to these standards?

The fourth and final pathway is the assessment pathway. In schools that have become sophisticated in the use of student assessment data I have found that they have also become involved in the analysis of the assessments used to obtain the data. This pathway has as many lanes as there are student assessments. Again, for simplification, a single box labeled "all assessments" is used.

Fortunate are those who have access to the standardized assessments or to the content maps upon which the assessments are built. I find it hard to understand why some states find it necessary to deny instructional staff access to the very assessments that are measuring what they are responsible for teaching. As a Federal Aviation Administration (FAA) certified flight instructor for hot air balloon pilots I had total access to all questions that my students would be asked on all FAA examinations. This is true of all pilots at all levels of proficiency. If it is good enough for the commercial multi-engine jet pilot then I fail to understand why we have to keep the third-grade reading assessment under wraps. There is so much to be learned from studying these exams, from creating parallel learning experiences and assessments, from matching instruction with curriculum with assessment. Study key words, concepts, and phrases used in assessments and understanding the relative weighting given to various content items in order to properly balance the school's own curriculum. School curriculum must not only be aligned with state requirements but also balanced in terms of time and emphasis. All of these things come from going down the assessment pathway and learning from the detailed results of the exam. Where staff does not have access to the results, other than a score, this becomes impossible, and a great deal of understanding and wisdom are lost.

Let's take a closer look at each of these pathways and some examples of how the analysis might proceed.

The first lane of the student pathway is that of the individual student. Individual student assessment data might be reviewed to determine level of proficiency and degree of need. If need is identified then certainly further study is required to specifically identify the specific help required, although this, sadly, is not always the case. Recently at a dinner party a teacher, not knowing my profession, was belaboring her woes as a type of resource room teacher who had responsibility for students assigned to her coming from grades 5 through 12 for help in as wide a variety of content areas as one could imagine. Some students were assigned for just a period or so for a few weeks, some for most of the day, and some for most of the year. From the conversation it appeared that her room served as nothing more than meeting some sort of paper requirement that the students be given extra help. She had lost all hope and was happy that the school year was about to end and she would be on to another job. This is just a single example. But I have no doubt similar situations exist in at least a few other places. The real need is to convert the data coming from the assessment to the wisdom of assigning the student to a place and time where he/she can benefit and gain the required proficiency. Likewise, the real organizational wisdom is in the ability to create such places. If remediation is required, it is essential that a "boiler plate rehash program" not be used but that instead a program be developed that targets the specific needs of each student.

If item analysis is to be used it must be used in conjunction with each assessment item's "p-score." Simply put p-scores are a decimal figure that indicates the percentage of students who responded positively to an assessment prompt. A p-score of 0.91, for example, indicates that 91% of students responding to the prompt answered correctly. Likewise a p-score of 0.15 indicates that only 15% of the students responded correctly to the prompt. P-scores are best amassed over a large region or even state. This gives them stability. Comparison of local p-scores against regional or state "p-scores" is a valid process that allows one to compare the relative difficulty of each assessment item. If, for example, in a region where 25,000 students were administered an exam and an item received a p-score of 0.10, the item should be seen as extremely difficult and as an item that would differentiate between those who were merely proficient and those who were advanced.

Without using the p-scores a district, or building, may look at their item analysis and see that only 20% of their students responded correctly to a prompt. This might in turn become an immediate focus of further instruction. However by looking at regional or state p-scores one might see that the regional score is a 0.09, meaning that only 9% of students in the whole region or state correctly answered this difficult question. So 20% is better when compared to the larger cohort and to the degree of difficulty indicated by the p-score and should not become an immediate red flag issue unless there is additional compelling information.

Another process along the individual student lane is that of reviewing the student's prior history and programmatic data. How long have they been in the district? Have they ever been retained? Have they ever been identified for special programs? Have they taken advantage of opportunities for remediation in the past? How early in the student's career can we identify the problem or success? What steps could or should have been taken at that time? Can we now identify students at that same point who may exhibit problems in the future? We can look at how the student is achieving across disciplines. Does the same lack of proficiency show up in other instructional areas? Is the lack of proficiency in one subject area caused by the lack of proficiency in another? What is the most important proficiency to focus upon? What can we learn from this student's value added profile; what has been the student's progress over time in this school?

One caveat should be mentioned at this point. Some assessments are not meant to measure individual student performance but rather are designed to best measure group performance. Oddly, these same assessments are used to determine who is required to receive additional instruction. The point here, however, is that it is unwise to push the use of individual assessment data far beyond its intended use. Individual assessment data is best when used in conjunction with other sources of information regarding the student's proficiency or mastery of subject matter. Information such as teacher-given grade, teacher observation, and other assessments are all useful in making an evaluation.

When dealing with cohorts of students, all of the factors mentioned above come into play. Although it is a different lane of the Student Pathway, the issues remain the same as do the types of analysis. Again, if item analysis of assessments is being used, it is essential to keep in mind the p-score for each item. Do we have sufficient data to look at the cohort over time? Can we see early warnings or signs of problems as we follow this cohort back upstream to early grade levels? Can we see points where earlier intervention could have been helpful? Can we see issues of ethnicity, socioeconomic level, gender, sending school or class, years in the system, or previous program history? Can we cross tab within the cohort to other subjects to see if there are general weaknesses or more specific areas of weakness? Does one area of weakness contribute to another? Can we take a look at the cohort's progress, or lack of it, over time?

We now focus upon the system or organizational pathway. An understanding of systems is necessary for all successful school improvement projects. Systems thinking is covered in Chapter 5 as one of four "key concepts." Allow me, however, to present a central thought regarding systems: Russell Ackoff taught me more than a decade ago, that "systems are not the sum of their parts but rather are a product of their interactions." So when we deal with school districts as systems we should not deal with the component parts as if they are separate items that can be summed in order to make a complete system, but rather that the system emerges when the separate parts are joined in such a way that their interactions focus on the system's purpose. This is true for each component part of the system, such as an elementary, middle, or high school. Although each of these three subsystems belongs to a larger system, the school district, they in turn are composed of many different subsystems, all of which must interact positively in pursuit of the system's purpose: the learning of all students.

So, the system pathway contains many lanes, but all of the lanes make use of data in similar ways for the purpose of improving learning for all students. In fact, using system data is not all that different than using individual and cohort student data. The numbers are larger, the focus is broader, individual students get lost in the vast array of program, grade level, building, and district data and we look for larger trends and comparisons, whether at the district, building, grade, or program level.

We look to item analysis, in conjunction with p-scores, for our strengths and weaknesses; we seek information regarding district demographics as well as using longitudinal district assessment data; we cross tab each assessment with assessments in other subject content. We include the process of disaggregation by demographic, programmatic, and process data, and we conduct value added analysis to determine student progress.

The benchmarking pathway contains three lanes: benchmarking against self; benchmarking against similar schools; benchmarking against local, state and/or national standards. As a high school student I participated in track. Back then my event was called the 440-yard run. It really was more of a long dash and took stamina and endurance that I had in short supply. Often, as I neared the last turn, I found myself so far back that no one appeared to be in front of me. Without benchmarking that can easily happen to poorly performing isolated schools that have no idea how others have already solved the problems they are facing. We are long since beyond the time when individual schools and districts can continue to operate in isolation without regard for the need to perform in accordance to state and national standards, and other school districts.

There are a variety of ways to establish benchmarking cohorts. As high school principal, I looked among the high schools within our athletic league that were similar in size, geographic location, and wealth (personal property and personal income). As superintendent I looked across a wider area for schools of equal size and wealth with similar budget history. As a consultant I looked, in one instance, for schools that were all situated in very remote regions of our state yet were very wealthy because they were very popular tourist destinations. These schools had small enrollments because the resident populations were small but their tax bases were high due to the many vacation homes and resorts. Although the characteristics of the districts within this benchmarking cohort were similar, they were located many miles from each other.

When benchmarking, we look at our strengths and weaknesses in terms of our self over time, in terms of what other similar schools have accomplished, and in terms of what our local, state, or national standards expect of us. We also seek to learn from similar schools that are out-performing us: what they do to achieve such results. I previously noted the concept of *frontier analysis* that deals exclusively with this last lane.

States require adequate yearly progress toward the achievement of proficiency and mastery in reading and mathematics. This too is analyzed at the district, building, or program level. In all three lanes, benchmarking against self, against similar schools, and against standards, longitudinal (historical) data is essential. Otherwise one still only has a snapshot rather than a video.

The final pathway is the pathway of the assessment itself. State and local school districts vary in the amount and type of assessment they perform. Some districts have moved to quarterly assessment in reading and mathematics with an assessment that measures progress toward expected end-of-school-year proficiency. There is, of course, the concern that we are assessing more than we are teaching. However, it is my belief that good assessment is necessary for good teaching. Has teaching taken place if learning hasn't? I don't think so. Good teaching requires continuous assessment and assessment takes places everyday and in many forms. As will be seen in Chapter 5, assessment of key indicators of student success should drive instruction.

What I judge to be school districts with the most sophisticated ability to use student assessment data have also turned their attention to the analysis of the assessments themselves. Because of the variation among states, a school district's ability to analyze assessments may be severely limited.

I presented a training session in one southern state where the tests were kept hidden from the teachers and even for educators to discuss the test was a crime. In such places the ability to make use of the assessments themselves as a tool for learning is just about impossible. Fortunately I live and worked in New York state, it provides a wide degree of information regarding its assessments. In fact, I coordinated regional scoring of English and mathematics exams for the 13 component school districts of our BOCES. Aside from allowing for the rapid scoring of exams it was one of the best in-service training processes for the classroom teachers who scored the region's exams and then returned to their own districts to share what they learned, not only about scoring but about student responses and the nature of the assessment itself. The ideal is for instructional content and methodology to match the standard and how it is assessed. It is also important that one come to understand the cognitive level of the assessment prompts (Bloom's Taxonomy) and integrate at least that level or higher into instruction. I cannot see how this can be accomplished in places where the assessment itself is kept under lock and key. Some are concerned about teaching to the test. But if the test indeed measures the standard it is also teaching to the standard!

Let's take a look at how some districts are viewing assessments. Some are given, or develop, an "item" map, which provides specific information regarding what part of the standard each item is attempting to assess. By looking at item maps over time, one can see changing emphasis by noting the number of items devoted to each part of the standard. Some districts have not been content with state issued item maps and have, on their own, analyzed each item to see if it truly assesses what the state says it does, and further, if it also measures some other part of the standard or a prerequisite skill. At least one region has developed, and shared, what is called a key phrase listing—the wordings that are used on the assessments with which students should become familiar. Typically these are prompts that students are required to accomplish. Assessments in one subject area are also reviewed to determine their dependency on proficiency in other subject areas. Finally, scoring of assessments is coupled with a process called error coding. Prior to scoring any exam an agreed upon number of error codes are established—perhaps four to six error codes for each exam. Error codes in math might be: did not understand the question, wrong process used, incorrect computation, and failure to answer. With error coding the school not only knows the score but also the pattern of errors displayed by its students.

It is not being suggested that all school districts make use of all pathways and all possible lanes at all times. Schools, however, that have spent many years going down the data road are now in position where they can indeed make use of any of these pathways and lanes in learning more about their system and in making truly databased decisions. Each dataset mentioned above has the ability to better inform each other dataset. Indeed, as each process is completed, a more complete "picture" of the issue emerges.

What, then, is the link between Dr. Victoria Bernhardt's model of "Multiple Measures of Data" presented in Chapter 2 and the model of "Data Pathways" presented above? Both models can be used to better understand the process of converting data to wisdom. Neither excludes the other. They can be used separately or together. The purpose of both models is to demonstrate how individual pieces of data must be used in conjunction with other pieces of data in order to convert data to wisdom. This often leads to the question: "When will we know when we have adequately explored a topic before reaching conclusions as to cause and remedy?" My best advice is that you will know when you arrive at that point. You will have the feeling that all possible avenues have been explored and that all possible wisdom has been squeezed from the data. Your team, group, committee will be in general agreement on that point. No available data stone will have been left unturned and you will recognize that you can move forward to the next step. Because we are educators and not engineers—we perhaps cannot be as exact in accounting for every last bit of evidence or running every last possible test, but we will arrive at a point where the data we have on hand has been sufficiently analyzed and converted to higher knowledge, understanding, and wisdom to enable us to move forward to decision making.

A suggestion was once made that perhaps the arrows in Figure 3.1 (see p. 45) should be pointing up instead of down. Although I will agree that the flow of communication will and ought to be multi-directional at all times, my simple model is based upon a single set of student assessment data that most typically arrives at central office, is broken apart and distributed to buildings, and then broken apart again and distributed to departments or individual teachers and grade levels. As the data is processed and analyzed, as described above, there will be calls for new datasets and a virtual web of cross chatter and up and down chatter should indeed result. For simplicity Figure 3.1 illustrates only the starting phase and is used as a basis for my discussion. It is not meant to establish any limitations to the web of communication that will ultimately develop as the dataset is converted to wisdom. Likewise, student report card data and attendance data, although gathered at the classroom level, are typically aggregated at the building or district level and then reported back down through the system.

A question is often raised regarding finding the time it will take for such data analysis to take place. I can only go back to Chapter 2 and the definition of Databased Decision Making which is: "a system of deeply rooted beliefs, actions, and processes that infuses organizational culture and regularly organizes and transforms data to wisdom for the purpose of organizational decisions." Where this is true:

♦ There will be time allocated

♦ There will be administrative leadership and understanding

♦ There will be Board of Education and community support

♦ There will be focused staff development on the use of data

♦ There will be staff specifically devoted to assist with data analysis

♦ There will be public accountability for results, and

♦ No part of the system will be left untouched or unchanged.

Summary

In this chapter I have presented and explained my concept of Data Pathways and the multiple ways in which they can be used to better illuminate student achievement within the context of a school district, building, or program. Each of the four pathways is composed of at least several lanes, each of which provides for more specific analysis of student achievement results. While not all pathways or lanes need to be used at all times, the more sophisticated a school becomes in making use of data in its decision making, the more use it will make of them. I have also briefly explored the relationship between "Data Pathways" and Dr. Bernhardt's "Multiple Measures of Data."

Questions to Think About

1. What "Pathways" does my system use in decision making?
2. What "Pathways" are not being used?
3. What is keeping my system from using all "Pathways" at least some of the time?
4. Are there are other data "Pathways" being used within your system that are not explained in this chapter? If so what are they? Please share them with the author.

4

Value-Added Analysis

The concept of applying "value-added analysis" (VAA) to student learning data is credited to Dr. William Sanders who, at the time he developed his ideas, was an agricultural statistician at the University of Tennessee. He reasoned that it was crucial to measure not only the academic achievement of students but their academic progress as well. Using the statistical methods developed by Dr. Sanders, the State of Tennessee began making use of value-added analysis as part of its "Educational Improvement Act" in 1992 and was the first state to do so (The Tennessee Value-Added Assessment System [TVAAS]). Dr. Sander's method uses data from the same student achievement assessments currently in use to determine individual student and cohort progress over time. Rather than a snapshot taken by the achievement test, VAA uses the data from the series of snapshots (data from achievement tests over time) to predict what student progress should be and then to determine what student progress has been. In addition, VAA screens out non-school variables leaving only the school's influences upon the progress measurement. While high achievement is to be prized, schools that show the greatest increases in student progress should be given the highest laurels.

More recently Dr. Sander's work has influenced pilot programs in Colorado, Iowa, Ohio, Pennsylvania, and New Hampshire. Pennsylvania's pilot is required as of 2007–2008. Many school districts have adopted the concept of VAA on their own with the support of SAS or other consulting agencies. The Milwaukee Public Schools, for example, have partnered with the Wisconsin-Madison Center for Educational Research (WCER) located at the University of Wisconsin-Madison's School of Education in the development of their own VAA process. The Value-Added Research Center (VARC) at WCER has also developed a network of schools using VAA in Wisconsin, Minnesota, and Michigan. The value-added research being conducted at VARC is being led by Dr. Rob Meyer. Battelle for Kids, located in Columbus, Ohio, is also a center of VAA and conducts workshops and facilitation while also producing training and instructional materials. Another VAA dissemination force is "Operation Education" located at The Center for Greater Philadelphia and directed by Theodore Hershberg. The Center maintains a good deal of information regarding VAA at it's website (see listing at the end of this chapter).

Interest in VAA is also found in New York State although no statewide initiative has as yet taken place. The New York State School Boards Association has championed VAA since 2003. Newly-elected Governor Spitzer is asking the State Education Department and its Board of Regents to establish a statewide VAA system and this may become reality within a short time. The Capital Region BOCES, under the leadership of Assistant District Superintendent for Instructional Services, Dr. Kathryn Gerbino, has, upon request, provided VAA services to any New York school district. To date, 20 school districts have requested such help. New York City, the largest district in the state, accounting for approximately 50% of the state's public school enrollment, is also moving toward utilization of VAA. Battelle for Kids, originally focused on helping schools in Ohio meet their instructional obligations using VAA, has also opened its resources to those across the country. Since its start in Tennessee in 1992, VAA is now more rapidly moving into the mainstream of educational accountability throughout the United States. Currently there are at least seventeen states that have at least some level of interest or program involving VAA.[1] Simple VAA spread to England in 1998 and was followed in 2004 with a much more robust VAA effort that has now become standard.

Dr. Sanders, although now retired from the University of Tennessee (2000), is continuing his active involvement with VAA as it rolls out and continues to develop across the nation. He has worked with many states and the federal government and has worked with colleagues to develop software systems to enable the creation of the value-added metric. Interestingly, Dr. Sanders is not an educator. Perhaps this is an advantage. His field of interest was primarily as an agricultural statistician. He now serves as manager for value-added assessment and research at the SAS Institute, Inc. located in Carey, North Carolina and also is a senior research fellow at the University of North Carolina.

Although there have been many articles written on VAA, and there are many resources on the Internet, I have found no books devoted solely to the topic and hence this chapter is offered as a primer for those seeking basic information, an overview of current usage and benefits, and a guide to further resources.

Perhaps my very first task is to define value-added analysis. Again we find that there are several terms that are all used roughly the same way. These are: value-added education, value-added assessment, value-added testing, value-added analysis, and value-added evaluation. For purposes of simplicity I will make consistent use of *"value-added analysis"* (VAA), which appears to be the most popular term if one relies upon the number of Google hits. I also think it has the added benefit of focusing upon the process of analysis rather than

1   http://www.cgp.upenn.edu/ope_nation.html

simply assessment or evaluation. The term value-added education is too indistinct or broad a term for my taste.

A basic definition coming from the Pennsylvania Value-Added Assessment System (PVAAS) is copied below. Interestingly they use *"value-added assessment"* as their systemic term and use *"value-added analysis"* in their definition. Perhaps proof positive that these terms are used interchangeably.

> Value-added analysis is a statistical method used to measure the influence of a district and school on the academic progress rates of individual students and groups of students from year-to-year."

Yet there is more to VAA than is provided above. Similar to our discussion in Chapter 2 regarding databased decision making, value-added analysis performs as a system and must be embedded within the total organization. And so I would add:

> and which performs as a system of deeply rooted beliefs, actions, and processes that infuses organizational culture and regularly transforms data to wisdom for the purpose of making organizational decisions for the purpose of improving student learning.

Before taking this definition and breaking it down by its key component parts, I think it is necessary to inform that value-added analysis is not just another system of measuring student achievement. It is a statistical process that uses individual student achievement scores, over time, to measure student *progress*. Figure 4.1 below will help explain this concept.

Figure 4.1. Value-Added Analysis: Conceptual Diagram

	Achievement	
	High Achievement Low Progress #1	High Achievement High Progress #2
	Low Achievement High Progress #4	Low Achievement Low Progress #3

Progress

(Concept adapted from a document at The Center for Greater Philadelphia's website on Value-Added Analysis)

In cell #1 we have high-achieving schools with poor student progress (growth). These schools are most often located in high wealth areas that rely upon their high test scores for accolades of distinction. In reality, however, students in these schools are born on third base and the schools think that they have hit a homerun. The fact that students in these schools progress below their capabilities is masked by their high achievement scores. These schools need to be shaken from their collective slumber and challenged to deliver instruction and programs that will enable their students to progress at much higher levels.

In cell #2 we find the schools that not only have high achievement (proficiency) but also demonstrate, through value-added analysis, that their students are also progressing at a high rate. These are the schools that truly deserve the accolades of distinction and they are the schools that should be modeled by schools in cell #1.

In cell #3 we find the truly dysfunctional schools. Students neither achieve well nor progress highly. These are the schools that are most certainly in need of identification and improvement.

In cell #4 we find schools that have a record of low achievement but high progress. These are typically the schools that are performing mightily on behalf of their students but such effort is often hidden by their low achievement scores. These schools are often located in the poorest of our neighborhoods and students come to school with multiple barriers before they ever begin to approach learning. Many of these schools can serve as models for schools in cell #3.

Once more, let's take a definition and break it down by its key component parts.

> Value-added analysis is a statistical method used to measure the influence of a district and school on the academic progress rates of individual students and groups of students from year-to-year and that performs as a system of deeply-rooted beliefs, actions, and processes that infuses organizational culture and regularly transforms data to wisdom for the purpose of making organizational decisions for the purpose of improving student learning.

Value-added analysis is a complex *statistical method*. VAA requires a large amount of coherent and clean data for each student. By coherent I mean that the various sets of data can work with each other in such a way that a student's progress and achievement can be tracked from year to year in each major subject area. Students must be tested at least annually on tests that employ a common scale. By clean, I mean that each set of data must include similar student identifiers and student ID and that the data is accurate and relatively complete over time. One of the things I found in working with school data in earlier years was that various datasets were not easily joined and that much of the data was inaccurate. My own hypothesis as to why this was so is that data had never really been used and hence the effort to make it accurate was seen as wasted energy. Also, because various datasets were never used in conjunction with each other there was no immediate need to make them relational. Typically, each dataset was established within a "silo" culture. Nothing short of a finely stocked and tuned data warehouse is required for VAA. Once such a warehouse is established, its use for VAA is highly sophisticated and typically requires the use of an outside contractor, such as SAS listed below. I am certainly not a statistician and will not attempt to explain the details of how VAA works statistically. Those interested in this information can find resources in the bibliography or in the resources listed at the end of this chapter. In fact, one criticism of VAA is that the statistical processes taking place in the "statistical black box" are subject to challenge. There is ample argument, however, in defense of the processes used. Prior to VAA there was no way by which to measure the effect schools had on student growth. Now, with VAA, there is a tool, perhaps no more perfect than the standardized achievement test, but a tool that has shown great promise in adding to the school improvement tool kit.

In addition to requiring large amounts of clean data, the data must be analyzed in a highly sophisticated manner that requires specialized knowledge that schools must find outside their own systems. This requires financial cost and trust as well as a high degree of communication between the service provider and the whole school staff.

One of the assurances of VAA is that it *measures the influence of a district and school* absent the influences of home and/or community environmental or cultural factors. Because it measures achievement over time, the longitudinal nature of the data used to predict progress is also more stable. With this assurance it is not only possible to measure the influence of a school district or school building but also, VAA claims, it is capable down to the classroom level. VAA data has been used to demonstrate what, as educators—we all believe—that teachers make a difference. Using VAA the differences in student progress among and between teachers becomes visible. For the first time we have the binocular ability to look at teacher's effectiveness not only through achievement and progress, but with lenses that filter out variances caused by factors other than instruction. In my mind, this new-found tool must be used in a climate of trust rather than in a climate of fear. It should become a tool for individual professional development, faculty growth, and mentoring rather than a tool for discipline and dismissal. Perhaps this is an ideal vision, but the more we approach this ideal the more we will become capable of true system improvement. In order to alleviate fear and distrust in its use, some jurisdictions, such as Pennsylvania, have guaranteed that it will not be used down to the classroom level. On the other hand, the State of Tennessee does make provision for the examination of progress down into the classroom level. I would hope, however, that regardless of state requirements, that instructional staff would take the initiative on their own once they "saw" what the VAA data had to show to use the data to improve instruction. We all now live in an environment of heightened accountability. It does not make sense that all in education are accountable with the exception of those in the classroom. It makes even less sense to those who work outside of education who face accountability issues as a normal part of their work-a-day life. VAA needs to be used as a tool to remedy cause and not as a weapon to assign blame. It needs to be used as a measure to celebrate progress when it happens and to focus resolve when it doesn't. In the long run, VAA can be the tool that enables the system to have the wisdom at its command to make the most appropriate decisions in the timeliest manner. For those interested in exploring the issue of VAA and teacher effectiveness further, I suggest the Winter 2004 issue of "Thinking K-16" (44 pp.) from The Education Trust noted at the end of the chapter.

In Chapter 5 I will explain what I believe to be four key concepts that must be understood and used in any successful school improvement effort. One of these is the concept of "system thinking." I believe that teacher effectiveness is essential for effective learning, but who is responsible for ensuring teacher effectiveness? Is it the individual teacher, the team, the principal, the superintendent, or is it the Board of Education? As I understand "system thinking," the responsibility for teacher effectiveness rests with the system and with those who primarily control it. If indeed through VAA, it is discovered that a specific teacher is not sufficiently effective, my questions are:

- ♦ Who supervised this teacher?
- ♦ Who supported this teacher?
- ♦ Who recommended this teacher for tenure?
- ♦ Who recommended this teacher for employment?
- ♦ Who interviewed this teacher?

I could continue on with many more questions. Even a teacher in a one room school house is embedded in a larger system, which has a certain amount of responsibility for the fact that he is there. This is why I believe VAA must be used in a broader sense than just focusing upon individual teachers and classroom groups. At the same time, however, I do not reject the idea that VAA data can identify teachers who are in need of improvement. What VAA reveals is much more often a "system" issue than an individual issue. Building reflective, collaborative, supportive systems will do much to enable individual teachers to grow toward excellence.

VAA measures and reports upon the academic progress rates of individual students and groups of students over time. Battelle for Kids(see Additional Resources at chapter's end) uses the term "The Power of Two: Progress and Achievement" as a type of mantra in their programs, conferences, and instructional materials. Educators have used achievement testing for many years to measure student proficiency but it is only relatively recently that many states and school systems have also begun to measure student progress. Indeed, our new-found ability to make statistical sense of these two measures provides a strong enabler for what I described in Chapter 1 as the sixth and most recent fundamental shift in American education—the greatly increased demand that schools be held accountable for student learning and that they work toward improved learning for all students.

We ask the same questions regarding progress as we ask about proficiency. Where do we find high and/or low progress in our system, what locations, departments, classes, cohorts, etc? Why are students, cohorts, classes, progressing or not progressing? We again use root cause analysis (RCA) to seek our answers and to identify points for intervention via improvement strategies. This can, and should, be accomplished on all levels, individual student, student cohorts, programs, processes, classes, departments, and schools.

We now come to the concluding clause of my definition, "which performs as a system of deeply rooted beliefs, actions, and processes that infuses organizational culture and regularly transforms data to wisdom for the purpose of making organizational decisions for the purpose of improving student learning." The deeper meaning of this clause was first put forth in the definition of Databased Decision Making (DBDM) found in Chapter 2. In essence: to be truly effective VAA must become part of how the school goes about its business. It enters into the values and beliefs of both the organization and its many members and results in daily actions and processes that enable improved progress and achievement for all students. These actions and processes can be found at all levels within the system: the district, the school building, programs and departments, and in classrooms. And, of course, the focus here is on the improvement of student learning.

The definition and function of VAA has been briefly explained. It is now appropriate to briefly explain its application and use in the school setting and most importantly in the school improvement process.

VAA provides a much needed array of missing information to all school databased decision-making processes from the district offices right across to the classroom. VAA data provides a clear picture of what is working (enabling student progress) and what is not working (not enabling student progress) and therefore allows better adjustment and or selection of policy and programs. When combined with information provided by achievement assessments it provides information necessary for both individual and cohort instructional decisions by teaching staff and others.

As shown in Figure 4.1, lack of student progress may be masked by high-achievement test scores. This needs to be known if the school is to "add value" to the student's learning curve. This is just as true for individual students as it is for cohorts and sub-groups. Likewise, when achievement is low but growth is high, the school needs to know that its work is paying off and that it needs to stay the course. Like all other datasets, value-added (VA) data will focus discussion on the issues being revealed and the VA data, when used with other datasets, will slowly transform to information, knowledge, understanding and wisdom that will enable the best possible decisions to be made. VA data, both positive and negative, should shed light upon school structures, processes, curricular and instructional practices, scheduling, assignment of resources, assignment of staff and such issues of student readiness.

VAA also opens the window into the realm of teacher effectiveness and the focusing of teacher development toward specific areas of need. Increasingly the role of effective and ineffective teachers has been shown to have crucial impact upon the progress of students and it therefore follows that VAA can provide essential information in identifying those teachers in need of assistance and those who are best able to give it. Some suggest that this concept should be extended into the compensation system for teachers. While many express fear of the misuse of VAA in the evaluation of teaching, and indeed states such as Pennsylvania have stopped at that threshold, other states such as Tennessee have long since used VAA in that capacity. Perhaps as VAA continues to develop and its use becomes more widespread, initial fears and misuse will diminish and increasing benefit can be achieved through its application to persistent problems.

The Pennsylvania Department of Education suggests the following uses for its value-added assessment system:

- Determine if a year's worth of growth was made at each grade level in reading and math;

- Identify which groups of students (advanced, proficient, basic, below basic) are making expected growth or are making more or less than the expected amount of growth in a given school year;

- Look at the progress and growth of different subgroups of students;

- Identify students at risk for not meeting proficiency on a future Pennsylvania System of School Assessment (PSSA);

- Use progress data with achievement data at parent/teacher conferences, and;

- Use progress data with achievement data to make local instructional and curriculum decisions.

In addition the Pennsylvania Department of Education (PDE) points out that with value-added analysis teachers are able to:

◆ Monitor the progress of all students, from low achieving to high achieving, ensuring growth opportunities for all students;

◆ Engage in professional dialogue with a focus on achievement and progress, and

◆ Begin grade-level discussions regarding instructional practices that result in higher levels of student growth.

The PDE also suggests that District administrators can use VAA to:

◆ Monitor building level progress;

◆ Engage staff at all levels to consider specific student concerns;

◆ Look at trends among disaggregate groups and develop strategies that address specific weaknesses, and

◆ Consider the influence of district resources and services on student progress.

The initial complexity of bringing VAA into a school system requires that the leadership be knowledgeable, implementation planning must be thorough, the assignment of resources sufficient for the task, and the timetable realistic. Awareness and training of key administrative staff and then engagement of all administrative staff are perhaps the essential first steps followed by the decision to become involved. In certain states this decision has already been made as the requirement has been laid upon the schools through regulations. Outsourcing of staff training, data analysis and reporting, and other aspects of the VAA program must be considered and resolved. Selection of a consulting agency is a crucial step and it seems as if few if any districts are in a position to avoid "going outside" in whole or in part on this issue. Instructional staff should be informed and involved as soon as possible regarding what role they will have and what the new data will mean for them and their students. Of course there is also the need to keep the community and parents informed, and where the move to VAA is not part of state regulation it will most likely come about only through Board of Education support and action, all of which will have to be developed long before any forward steps can be taken. The way in which all of these issues are dealt with will vary as much from district to district as will the district's local history, politics, climate, and character and abilities of its leadership.

Following the decision to move forward, the implementation of the plan must be constantly monitored and modified as new needs emerge. New staff positions may need to be created. One district established a "District Value-Added Specialist" position and filled it from among its instructional staff. This person worked as a "teacher of teachers" in helping them to initially develop a basic understanding of VAA and then to move on to ever greater knowledge of its uses as a tool to adjust individual and group instruction. Others have found the need to establish positions of data analyst or data specialist.

Over the last decade American schools have made great progress in both their awareness of and their actual use of student data to improve learning. The use of VAA will likewise not become integrated into all American schools overnight. It will be a process that will take more than several years within any one school district and more than that across any one state. Gradually, however, the concept of VAA will assume its place as one of the reliable tools which foster better databased decisions that enable improved learning for all students.

Summary

In Chapter 4 I have provided a definition and explanation of the Value-Added Analysis (VAA) concept as well as a brief overview of its historical development and present day usage. VAA measures student "progress" or growth and when combined with traditional assessment metrics that measure proficiency or achievement we get a much better definition of a school's effectiveness in enabling students to learn. VAA provides the necessary "power of two" as a means of accurately reporting and providing a basis for school accountability as well as providing "binocular vision" of individual student performance, growth and achievement. Some sample applications of VAA data to school improvement efforts have also been provided.

Questions to Think About

1. Am I able to explain the difference between student "progress" and "achievement" to a parent or non-educator friend?

2. Am I able to explain the fundamentals of VAA to a parent or non-educator friend?

3. If I was given VAA data for my classroom, how would I want to use it?

4. How would I want VAA data to be used in my school? In my school district? In my state? In the news media?

Additional Resources

Readers are invited to explore value-added analysis further by visiting the following websites:

Battelle for Kids, 1160 Dublin Road, Suite 100, Columbus, Ohio, 43215 http://www.battelleforkids.com/home The Value-Added Learning Network http://www.value-addedlearningnetwork.org/

Council of Chief State School Officers, One Massachusetts Avenue, NW Suite 700, Washington, DC 20001-1431 Web page on Growth Models http://www.ccsso. org/projects/accountability_systems/Growth_Models/

SAS: Government & Education, 101 SAS Campus Drive, Cary, NC, 27513 http:// www.sas.com/govedu/edu/index.html

The Center for Greater Philadelphia: Operation Public Education, 3701 Chestnut St., Philadelphia, Pennsylvania, 19104, VAA pages http://www.cgp.upenn.edu/ ope_value.html

The Education Trust, 1250 H St. NW, Suite 700, Washington, DC 20005 http://www2.edtrust.org Winter 2004 issue of "Thinking K-16" http://www2. edtrust.org/NR/rdonlyres/5704CBA6-CE12-46D0-A852-D2E2B4638885/0/Sprin g04.pdf .

The Value-Added Research Center, 1025 W. Johnson St., Suite 785, Madison, Wisconsin, 53706 http://varc.wceruw.org/researchAreas/network.php

5
Key Concepts

At the conclusion of a two day training session in the mid-west one of the participants asked a question that I had not been asked before. I was asked to sum up the most important aspects of the two days of training in several words. With just a moments hesitation I responded with: "systems thinking, key indicators of student success, databased decision making and root cause analysis." While on the flight home I realized that these four concepts deserved their own chapter and would serve later as the much needed foundation for presenting my ideas in Chapter 6 on what I have come to call Dynamic Planning.

It is my intent to share my thoughts on each of these concepts here as I think they are essential for all leaders of successful school improvement efforts. The Appendices contain a simple tutorial on each concept that may be used for staff-development purposes. While each of these topics can be pursued in much greater depth I think initially, it is proper for leaders to proceed with just a general operational understanding of each concept while developing their deeper understanding through direct experience and further reading.

Systems Thinking

I learned from Russell Ackoff that a system is not the sum of its parts but rather the product of the interaction of the parts. As a reminder I keep a small plastic box containing watch parts on my desk. Yes, it is at my left hand as I write. The box contains all the parts of a completely disassembled wrist watch. It will never function again as a system, yet all of the system parts are there. Putting a new battery into the box will not allow it to function. Placing a new quartz crystal in the box will do no better. The sum of the parts in the box does not equal a watch. The watch will only perform for its intended purpose when the parts are assembled in such a way that they can interact to meet the function of telling time.

In many ways school districts are similar to my box of watch parts. They are a collection of disassembled parts. We have buildings, departments, programs, many of which do not "speak" to each other. Some have likened this to programs being within "silos"—never having contact with other "silos" within the same district. In order for the system to better perform its function of enabling all students to learn, the parts have to interact in such a way that they are connected and aimed at the goals of the district. I was asked by a superintendent to work with his district on the improvement of their K-12 mathematics test scores. He convened a K-12 committee to work with me. It was the first time that representatives of K-12 teachers in this small district met to discuss mathematics. This was in a district where the teachers were all within the same small complex of buildings.

A simple system is composed of just three parts: some form of input, a process, and some form of output. I suppose we could look at a simple educational system in the following manner:

Inputs	♦ Time	♦ Materials
	♦ Student	♦ Method
	♦ Teacher	♦ Content
	♦ Place	
Process	♦ Instruction	♦ Assessments
	♦ Teaching	
Outputs	Student Learning:	
	♦ Dispositions	♦ Knowledge
	♦ Beliefs	♦ Skills
	♦ Values	♦ Behaviors
	♦ Understandings	

Of course school districts are usually much more complex, and consist of many more parts in the form of inputs, processes, and outputs but the principle remains that all aspects of the system can be broken down into one of the three categories. W. E. Deming is quoted as saying: "If you can't describe what you are doing as a process, you don't know what you're doing." Everything we do is process. My writing this book is a process. Teaching is a process. A single process is a simple system. A complex system, such as a school, is composed of thousands of processes. Hopefully, each is linked in such a way as to aid the system in meeting its ultimate purpose.

Systems nest within systems: leaf/tree/forest or class/school building/district. Systems thinking is about seeing the whole and being able to define "What is my system?" Every part of the system impacts all other parts of the system. In one large metropolitan area, for example, they found that the timetable for their teacher recruiting efforts was so delayed that it invariably left them recruiting among the leftovers rather than from the whole barrel of potential applicants. You cannot change one part of a system without impacting all other parts of the system.

Systems thinking is doing what is best for the system, not necessarily for its individual parts. Russell Ackoff pointed out that you could not take all of the best car parts in the world and put them together to make the best car because they simply were not designed to fit each other. Schools can easily become a conglomeration of "best practices" that do not fit each other simply through neglect to properly align them. We cannot expect the improvement of parts to be especially productive in improving the system when the connections among and between them are neglected. In fact, it will be counterproductive.

Once one can "see the system" and becomes a system thinker, it is impossible to go back to the world of bits and pieces. The insanity of it all is that most of our districts consist of bits and pieces and a systems thinker can go nearly insane before the district begins its process of assembly toward a true system. Leadership for school improvement must make "seeing the system" happen.

Several years ago I was interviewed by a school board as part of the consultant selection process. I explained that although I was probably seen as a relatively good high school principal, in retrospect much of what I did was at the expense of the K-12 system I was in. Because of my longevity and knowledge of which buttons to push I was able to hoard school district resources in terms of personnel and budget—in effect taking them from both the elementary and middle school levels. One board member asked if I would be different now that I understood systems. I replied something to the effect that I probably wouldn't change how I operated. He was obviously bothered and asked why. I responded that the expectations for the role of high school principal and the evaluation process all focused on how I performed as high school principal, not how I performed as a systems player. I had few obligations to the K-12 system and many for the proper functioning of the high school. Yes, I got the job as facilitator.

While facilitating a school-district team the high-school principal, who had been an elementary principal in the same district, shared that had he been a high school principal first, he would have been entirely different as an elementary school principal. It makes one wonder about our whole process of certification and pigeonholing people at one level or another for a good part of their professional careers. Or, as educators do we do it to ourselves? How eager are classroom teachers to change assignments to new grade levels or subject areas, even within their own area of certification? Certainly there is advantage to be gained from experience, but there is also advantage to be gained from new vantage points and experiences. How can we balance these issues for the benefit of both the system and the individuals within it? How much of "teacher burn-out" is caused by being in the same location, doing the same thing year in and year out? In New York we have over 700 independent school districts. A move from one district to another results in the complete loss of seniority, tenure, and placement on the salary schedule. Yet the local postal clerk can move from one state to another without loss of such job benefits. We need to look closely at the system we have created to see how it limits our personal and organizational freedom to grow.

One winter morning I approached the steps of my school before sunrise. The sky was still a deep winter blue with only the brightest stars able to overcome the growing light of the sun. I paused and looked up to the east and saw Venus—the brightest object in the sky. But then there was also Mars to be seen overhead and if my memory serves me well Jupiter was also in sight. And I realized that I was standing on yet a fourth planet—Earth—and suddenly nearly the whole of our Solar System became apparent as it slowly revolved around the soon to be seen Sun. I stood transfixed, seeing and feeling the planetary system for the first time. Such is the magic of truly "seeing" systems.

What does it feel like to truly "see" the full extent of your school system? How about the linkages between and among all of its levels and parts? What about the numerous interfaces between the school system and the external systems that either serve it or depend upon it? How does the school system relate to the local community college? What can be learned from the local community college regarding the students sent to it by the school system? What is the relationship between the local school system and the local Department of Social Services? Is the Superintendent on a first name basis with the Commissioner? How does the school district relate to the business community? There are a multitude of internal and external issues of connections. "A system is not the sum of its parts, but rather the product of the interaction of its parts." The parts interact through linkages, connections, communications, relationships, proper alignments, and certain tangibles that serve to lubricate, such as goodwill, trust, common vision, and goals.

I recently attended a conference where I was presenting on the concept of root cause analysis. The conference was a regional event, sponsored for school district leadership teams. From all signs, it was a very positive experience with many positive sessions, yet there was an underlying theme, I think, that kept the financial folks, the school business managers, away from the sessions where the school educational leaders were participating. Now there is a certain logic to this; I wouldn't want to sit through a 2-hour session on the finer points of the latest state aid reimbursement requirements perhaps anymore than a business manager may want to sit through a 2-hour session on the details of organizing a reading recovery program. But I do think it necessary, in fact essential, that the function of business manager not be excluded from the discussions involving the larger issues of the future directions and goals of the organization down to a certain level of detail. I have been fortunate to know and to work with, a good number of excellent business managers that had a seemingly magical touch in their ability to "find" funds for projects that they *knew about, were involved in,* and *thought were important.* Hence, it becomes a decision as to when and at what level to bring the business manager in. As a general rule of thumb I suggest that the business manager should never be in the dark about any program within the district, particularly regarding a program of any size, such as value-added analysis. Assignment of resources is essential and all resources require funding and budgeting. I recall the story of a teacher that was sent by her principal to a summer training program for the purpose of introducing a new science curriculum. She labored all summer learning the curriculum, was excited to start in September, and was paid by the district for her efforts. When she checked her room in August for the required equipment and supplies she found none. Inquiring further, she found that they had not been ordered by the business office as the funding was cut to meet budget requirements. Neither the principal nor the teacher had been informed. Where was the system? What kind of damage was done? How could it be remedied and by whom? Of course, such things do not happen often. Do they? All people need to be part and feel part of the system.

This leads to people that we might classify as auxiliary staff but are really some of the key players in the lives of our students. The first and last person to greet and leave our students is often the bus driver who the picks them up and drops them off at home. These are important folk. So are those who work in the cafeteria. If it is true that "an army marches on its stomach" (Napoleon Bonaparte), then I think it is equally true that a positive school climate is at least partially the result of the food served and the attitude of the staff in its cafeteria. In my own years as high school principal I experienced a positive change in student behavior when we were able to enlarge the size of the cafeteria, provide additional serving lines that enabled faster service, offer more diverse choices, provide smaller tables and booths rather than longer traditional feeding troughs, provide access to bathrooms from within the cafeteria rather than from down the hallway, and changed the schedule in such a manner that there was a 10-minute interval between lunch periods allowing the cafeteria to be cleaned and the trash barrels to be emptied before each session. And yes, I think the cafeteria staff was generally friendly toward the students. Custodial and maintenance staff are also important folks around the building from fixing the big ticket items like power outages to helping a student with a stuck locker. Office and secretarial staff must deal with so much, students, staff, parents, and their bosses. Yet they are often the face of the school that are most remembered and they are the first voice on the phone. These people are all essential parts of the system and need to be informed, not only of the importance of their functions, but of their role in helping the district meet its goal—the improved learning of all its students.

Systems thinking is essential for successful school improvement efforts. Otherwise school leaders are left working with the bits and pieces, or school parts, and the improvement of one part may serve to make other parts more dysfunctional. School leaders should sit back and study their system, get to know it through observation and the analysis of data, (*data to information to knowledge to understanding to wisdom*) begin to ask questions, learn from those within the system, encourage others to "see" the system. While all of this can be done at the program or departmental levels, the power of systems thinking becomes greater as one moves up to the building and district levels. There is great power within a school district that has committed itself to systems thinking.

Key Indicators of Student Success

A key indicator of student success (KISS) is a student-focused measurable result that the school has the ability, desire, or need to influence and for which it is willing, or required, to be held accountable. Figure 5.1 below provides a visual overview of the narrative on key indicators of student success.

Figure 5.1. Key Indicators of Student Success

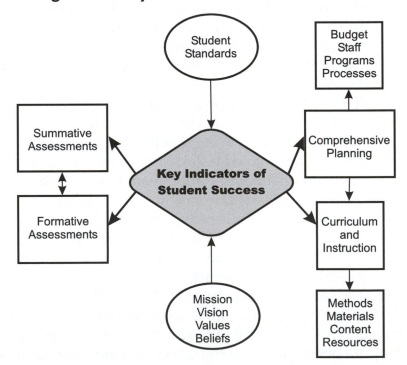

Because of NCLB there has been greatly increased focus on student proficiency in the areas of mathematics and English language. There has been a smaller NCLB focus on proficiency in the areas of science and social studies. While this newfound focus on these critical skill areas is necessary, the danger is that the focus becomes so narrowed that other essential aspects of a truly holistic education are pushed to the side and soon forgotten, or taken for granted. Here is where the development of KISS for each of these areas provides a means of maintaining focus on the broad spectrum of necessary student skills rather than upon only those required by NCLB.

An example of skills required for American workers in the 21st century is contained in the Secretary's Commission on Achieving Necessary Skills (SCANS) report published in 1991. The Commission identified five areas of basic competency:

♦ **Resources:** identifies, organizes, plans, and allocates resources;

♦ **Interpersonal:** works with others;

♦ **Information:** acquires and evaluates information;

♦ **Systems:** understands complex interrelationships;

♦ **Technology:** works with a variety of technologies.

The Commission then identified a three-part foundation of necessary skills and personal qualities. The three are:

♦ Basic skills,

♦ Thinking skills, and

♦ Personal qualities.

The SCANS report is a fine example of the full range of required skills and could be used as a basis, for the development of KISS. Perhaps these skills are harder to monitor and evaluate, but that should not be a cause for neglecting them. Detailed information regarding the SCANS report can be found at: http://wdr.doleta.gov/SCANS/

I know that some vocational schools have made use of the SCANS report in moving the report's content into the mainstream of vocational instruction and that vocational graduates are the better for it. The process involved taking the SCANS recommendations and integrating them into the instructional programs of the various vocational courses within the school. While the basic outline of the SCANS recommendations is a natural for vocational courses, the devil is in the details, and the details provided in the report enabled instructors to more easily integrate the full meaning of the report into their instructional program. Although this report is over 15-years old it was prepared with the idea of outlining skills for the 21st Century and I think it is still a timely document. For those interested in something more recent, the Partnership for the 21st Century has completed a "Framework for 21st Century Learning" that is available at their website referenced at the end of the chapter.

Without firm identification of KISS all the processes of a school tend to drift. KISS must drive all that takes place within the school district. KISS serves to align school processes toward their achievement.

Key Indicators:	◆ Anchor instruction
	◆ Make standards both visible and measurable Identify what the school sees as important
	◆ Enable measurement of school effectiveness
	◆ Define the purpose of school in measurable terms
	◆ Clarify which data is important and calls for analysis
	◆ Enables focused school improvement efforts
Key indicators are driven by:	◆ District vision, mission, values and beliefs
	◆ Required state and/or federal student standards
Key indicators drive:	◆ Curriculum and instruction
	◆ Including: methods, materials, content, resources
	◆ Comprehensive planning*
	◆ Including: budget, staffing, programs, processes
	◆ Formative and summative assessments

*In Chapter 6, I propose that a "Dynamic-Planning" process be considered as an improvement upon Comprehensive Planning, but for now, I will continue to use the generic term Comprehensive Planning.

An example of how a key indicator of student success is used is presented below. A worksheet template has been provided in the Appendices for use in identification and measurement of key indicators of student success.

Key Indicator	*Student Graduation Rate*
Desired Ideal Condition	100% of entering ninth-grade cohort will ultimately receive a high school diploma
Present Condition	84% of entering ninth-grade cohort receives a high school diploma
Gap	16% of entering ninth-grade cohort does not receive a diploma
Is this a Priority Issue?	Yes!
Goal Statement	Over the course of the next four years the percentage of the ninth-grade cohort who graduate with a diploma will increase from 84% to 100%

The *key indicator*, student graduation rate, enables the exposure of the present condition in terms of the ideal and presents the gap. The *key indicator* enables discussion regarding the gap and its importance as well as the development of a specific goal statement that can be measured over time.

"Goal Statements" must be ends-focused—in other words—they must be focused on the key indicator of student success. They must also contain a specific target for achievement, or progress, compared to the present as well as a timeframe for achievement of the target.

Next steps in the process of school improvement should include:

♦ Search and identification of the root cause(s) for the gap

♦ Selection of strategies for improvement (dissolving the root cause(s))

♦ Implementation of the strategies

♦ Monitoring of the implementation

♦ Evaluation of results (did the strategies make a difference)

Those who are leading a school improvement process need to become familiar with the concepts surrounding the identification of key indicators of student success and their implementation. Key indicators allow one to bypass the data swamp by pointing to specific datasets that must be monitored. Key indicators allow one to focus on ends rather than just the means. Through personal observation, I have seen where many school improvement processes become means focused, a listing of correlates or perhaps a listing of attributes of quality schools. These are all well and good, and some may indeed turn up in the search for root cause(s), however, the primary focus must remain on the identification and measurement of "student-focused measurable results." Of course, means are necessary to achieve all ends, but they should not overpower the sustained focus toward achievement of the goal.

Databased Decision Making

Although this key concept was discussed in detail in Chapter 2, here are a few additional comments. Perhaps no other recent change within education has been as great as the conversion of schools to utilizing data. As stated in the Introduction, I view this as the most recent of six fundamental shifts in public education. A Google search of the term "databased decision making" yielded 104-million results within a quarter of a second. Within a fifth of a second, a Google search the term "data-driven decision" found over 31.6-million results. Many of these citations dealt specifically with the use of data in education. We are in an era when data is now expected to be collected and used to improve learning for *all* students. Educators are expected to be agile in using data and being accountable for results. Much of this is a far cry from Statistics 101 and many educators today have earned their data battlefield commissions through in-the-trenches experience over the last several years. The fortunate few have been aided by having direct access to a data analyst who is familiar with not only statistics, testing, and measurement, but also with the needs of educators.

W. Edwards Deming has been quoted as saying "if you don't have data, you are just a person with an opinion." Jim Leonard said "In God We Trust, all others need data." We have moved into a data-driven century. Educators are perhaps among the last of all to be faced with the consequences of not being prepared for this new data-based world and many have been dragged kicking and screaming into it. However, it is obvious that great progress has been made over the last five years. Where there was once data illiteracy there is now a good deal of data wisdom. Where there was once no staffing to support this function we now find increasing numbers of data analysts working side by side with school leaders in making proper use of data for school improvement.

Russell Ackoff pointed out that you really can do very little with a single piece of data. Data must be converted to information, and then information converted to knowledge. Knowledge needs to be converted to understanding and understanding needs to be converted to wisdom. Using his formula of ten teaspoons of data for every teaspoon of information, we reach the conclusion that we need a million teaspoons of data to arrive at the level of one teaspoon of wisdom. Nevertheless, the best data-driven decisions are made at the levels of understanding and wisdom.

In my experience as a trainer, consultant, and facilitator I have seen numerous instances where the team I am working with has become "hooked" on data. This process usually starts when something completely new is exposed by a dataset or when commonly held assumptions are disproved. It is as if a totally new window is opened with a view never before seen. I remember a team of high school English teachers who came to their planning session convinced that class attendance was a factor in students achieving proficiency. The data revealed, however, that attendance was not a factor and in fact, if there was any tendency at all it was that the higher achieving students had a slightly higher rate of absenteeism. The team then began asking all sorts of questions that only the datasets could reveal and in short time they became "data sponges." My problem was that the only data manipulation ability we had was my going home and cranking out the cross tabulations by hand. I will deal more with this concern in Chapter 7, Making It Happen.

Perhaps if I had thought just a moment longer at the conclusion of that mid-western training session I would have added a fifth key concept—but then—it probably is more easily associated with databased decision making. The concept is variation. All systems and processes vary. All school data contains variation. The understanding of variation is essential for the proper use of data.

There are traditional ways of statistically describing variation, such as standard deviation. I have found another concept to be highly workable and illuminating. This is the concept of statistical process control (SPC). There are two types of variation.

♦ *Common cause variation* is a natural part of the system or process.

♦ *Special cause variation* is the result of a special, infrequent event or circumstance that is typically outside of the normal process.

I will use a simple example. In driving to work each day my trip takes on average, somewhere between 10 and 12 minutes. I know I am so fortunate to be so close to the office. The normal variation would perhaps be somewhere in the neighborhood of 2 or perhaps 3 minutes. However on one day it took me 30 minutes to drive to work. This would be flagged as special cause as it is far outside the boundary of normal variation. A bit of research shows that the delay was caused by my being stopped for a traffic violation (not really—just an example). It is the same with school data. I was working with a district-wide school improvement team; we were discussing student assessment data over the past several years. In one previous year in one of the elementary schools, there was a noticeable decline in student proficiency at a specific grade level. I began to question the team and it soon became obvious that for them it was past history, the cause had been discovered and eliminated and their strong attitude was one of "let's move on." As this was not the primary focus of our work, and because the signals to move on were so strong, move on we did.

Special cause variation in a school's assessment data, from one year to the next, may be due to one or more of the following or similar issues:

♦ Faulty or inappropriate test administration or testing conditions;

♦ Tampering with student responses or answer sheets;

♦ Significant changes in instructional staff or procedures;

♦ Significant emotional event, such as death of a student or staff member near the time the assessment was taken;

♦ Significant student-health related issue impacting numbers of students;

♦ Significant changes in student enrollment from one year to another in terms of demographic factors, size of cohort, length of time in district, etc.;

♦ Significant change in how the school went about working to improve student learning.

It should be noted that some of the special causes above could result in either positive special cause variation (improved student assessment scores) or negative special cause variation (lower student assessment scores).

When benchmarking an individual school's normal variation pattern within the normal variation pattern of the larger district, it may be found, for example, that the range of variation for this individual school is so extreme as to be seen as "special cause" within the context of the larger district. It then becomes obvious clear that "special cause" factors are within this school and that these must be dealt with in order to bring its variation under control in terms of the larger district. Several additional factors should be added to those above as possible causes for this wider variation:

♦ School building culture and climate, values and beliefs;

♦ School building leadership;

♦ School building staff development or lack of it;

♦ School building history.

Before a process of school improvement can truly begin, special cause variation has to be eliminated or severely reduced. If not, the system is really out of control begging the question: how can one begin to improve a system that is not in control? Once the system is in control and all variation is considered to be within the normal range, only then can the school improvement process proceed to reduce normal variation while moving the district higher on the ladder of expectations (KISS).

In Chapter 7, I make the plea for statistical assistance for the processes of data analysis, storage, retrieval, and presentation. Typically the people who enter the data and run the computers are not necessarily the people who are skilled in statistical analysis. Likewise, those of us who need to use the analysis are not often skilled in statistical analysis (at least something more in-depth than Statistics 101 & 102). The position of data analyst becomes the intermediary between the input of data, its analysis, and its presentation for use. The data analyst knows how to answer the questions being asked and also has a sense of what data and what format to use in presenting it to various constituent groups.

Root Cause Analysis

Root cause analysis (RCA) is the process of identifying "the deepest underlying cause, or causes, of positive or negative symptoms within any system, which, if dissolved, would result in elimination, or substantial reduction of the symptom."[1] Preuss, Paul (2003). *A School Leaders Guide to Root Cause Analysis*. Larchmont, NY: Eye On Education.

RCA is the final of our list of key concepts that are essential for all leaders of successful school improvement efforts. To reiterate, they are:

- systems thinking
- key indicators of student success (KISS)
- databased decision making (DBDM)
- root cause analysis (RCA)

Each of these four key concepts are related to each other and lean upon each other forming a whole system of thinking. It is not a surprise, therefore, that the foundation for a proper RCA rests upon the other three key concepts.

Why must school leaders mandate the search for root cause? The reasons are multiple:

- RCA helps dissolve the problem, not just the symptom.
- RCA eliminates patching and wasted effort.
- RCA conserves scarce resources.
- RCA induces discussion and reflection as well as the melting of pre-formed inaccurate judgments.
- RCA provides the rationale for strategy selection.

There are four modalities of RCA. They are:

- **Negative Reactive** identifies roots for existing problems.
- **Negative Proactive** identifies roots of future problems.
- **Positive Reactive** identifies roots for existing successes.
- **Positive Proactive** identifies necessary roots for future success.

We are most frequently engaged in the negative reactive modality. In fact, I have had friendly arguments with other "rooticians" over the efficacy of the other three modalities, some saying that you can only learn from things that have gone bad in the past. I completely reject that because I know that I have learned from my successes and have attempted to use this proactively to develop successful programs for the future. I encourage all school leaders to ex-

---

1 Preuss, Paul (2003). *A school leader's guide to root cause analysis*. Larchmont, NY: Eye On Education.

pand their use of RCA to cover all four modalities, realizing that the emphasis is to focus on the negative reactive mode.

Root causes are also found in a great variety of locations within a school system. There are at least four levels in which causation can be identified. These are:

♦ The incident or procedural level: We look for the cause of a specific incident or something related to a specific procedure. This is RCA at its simplest.

♦ The programmatic or process level: Here we look at a much wider arena of possible causation, but the RCA process still has rather narrow boundaries.

♦ The systemic level: This is the largest and widest arena for the search as it contains the whole of the organization. Because many root causes are found far from the symptom, one might begin a RCA process at the incident level and quickly move up to the level of the system. In fact, W. Edwards Deming taught that 85% of all problems are caused at the top of the system as the leaders are the ones who control the system. But it is wise not to make mountains of a mole hills while also remaining aware that some mole hills might be mountains in disguise.

♦ The external level: This is often the most difficult to deal with as the school only has slight ability to control many external factors. Schools often have enough problems of their own without attempting to solve external issues as well. I have had at least two very productive experiences, however, where I as a school leader, became deeply engaged in external issues. The first was within a regional Business–Education Council whose primary focus was supporting schools in their effort to improve student knowledge of economics and business. The second was as a member of a county-wide Department of Social Services–BOCES partnership focusing on the concept of developing a single point of entry for families into the wide variety of public social service programs.

There are a good number of tools that can be used to seek root cause. Among them are the:

♦ questioning data process,

♦ diagnostic tree,

♦ creative root cause analysis team process,

♦ five whys,

- force field analysis, and

- barrier analysis.

My previous text, the *School Leaders Guide to Root Cause Analysis: Using Data to Dissolve Problems* contains all that is necessary to get started with RCA. Additionally, I have placed a brief RCA tutorial in the Appendices. The point here is that before strategies for improvement are selected, the target for the strategies to attack must be identified and clearly stated. Improvement strategies must target the root cause, not the symptom. Strategy selection prior to root cause identification is a waste of resources where only excellent luck will result in success.

Summary

In this chapter I have discussed four concepts that I consider to be key understandings for all leaders of school improvement efforts. The four key concepts are: systems thinking, identification of key indicators of student success, databased decision making, and root cause analysis. Within the process of using data to arrive at decisions are the processes of converting raw data to information, knowledge, understanding, and wisdom, as well as the testing of data for variation in order to determine if the variation is normal or special cause.

Questions to Think About

1. Am I working in a system or in a collection of school parts? If a system: What can I do to strengthen the system? If a collection of school parts: What can I do to help make it more of a system?

2. Do I know what the Key Indicators of Student Success are for my school context? If not, how can I identify them?

3. Do I understand the difference between normal and special cause variation and why it is important to know the difference? How can I find out if the variation is special or normal?

4. When I am in a group attempting to deal with a problem do we stop and try to identify the "root cause"? If not, why not? If not, how can this change?

Additional Resources

Peter Senge's *The Fifth Discipline: The Art and Practice of the Learning Organization* is still a great text, even after 15 years. I typically read texts quickly, however, this text was so rich that I could mentally digest only small portions at a time. The five disciplines upon which Senge hangs his text are: Personal Mastery, Mental Models, Building a Shared Vision, Team Learning, and *Systems Thinking.*

Partnership for the 21st Century, 177 N. Church Avenue, Suite 305 Tucson, AZ 85701
    Framework for 21st Century Learning http://www.21stcenturyskills.org/

6
Dynamic Planning

Schools and school districts are under intense pressure to meet student standards imposed by state and national governments. Failure to meet these standards can often result in severe consequences for schools, their leaders, and staff. Schools have both limited resources and limited time to develop processes of continuous improvement that will allow them to move steadily toward established standards. Often, plans designed to help improve results are static documents that become little more than "shelf art" and become outdated soon after completion. Instead of helping, they become cumbersome additions to a school's already overloaded capacity to perform and provide further evidence of a system's dysfunction. Static plans are simply no longer capable of meeting the demands of a dynamic world.

Recently, I learned a new word while engaged in a completely different context than writing this book. The word's implication for what I was trying to share fascinated me and several hours were spent in researching its history and usage. The word is **akrasia**. It is a Greek word meaning "weakness of will." Akrasia was the Greek Goddess of distraction and her name is the basis for our English word "crazy"." More recently psychologists have revived the term to describe the action people take to engage in high-risk behavior when much safer alternatives are available. Some modern uses of the term also imply that the high-risk behavior is engaged in even though the safer alternative is well known. The example of smoking is given—where a person intellectually knows that smoking is a high-risk behavior, yet continues to make that choice—evidencing a "weakness of will". This akratic action is the same for all kinds of high-risk addictions. There perhaps is a duality within the akratic person or group that suggests that they know the harmful nature of their actions and that they believe that they will not suffer the consequences (magic thinking). In the book, edited by Robert J. Sternberg, *"Why Smart People Can Be So Stupid"* the point is made that smart people can succumb to akrasia at the same rate as less-smart people. Without belaboring the point, I believe that school improvement planning that does not make use of Databased Decision Making (DBDM) is akratic planning. Its participants are demonstrating "weakness of will" while knowingly engaging in high risk behavior in the hope that they will not suffer the consequences of their actions. It is also akratic in that it is probably an addiction. "We have always done it this way." Does anyone in American education today not know that the effective use of data is the key to improving schools? The risks of not using data properly are:

◆ wasted time and effort by those involved as well as by organization,

◆ wasted resources,

◆ loss of good will due to the preceding items, and

◆ loss of opportunity to improve learning for students.

The paragraphs that follow describe dynamic planning as a process that uses DBDM that enables schools to continually focus on the improvement of student learning while avoiding akrasia.

The concept of Dynamic Planning is the provision of an open and continuous planning process that can successfully deal with the increasingly dynamic demands being placed upon schools. Dynamic planning, in both concept and process, integrates the planning process into the core of how the school goes about its daily business. Instead of being an "add-on" dynamic planning consolidates, enhances, and sometimes replaces traditional processes, which can no longer serve to rapidly move the school toward mandated performance standards.

Perhaps a simple example is needed to demonstrate how present school processes inhibit dynamic reaction. In many school districts budget request forms are issued for the following school year prior to the end of December. This is a full 6 months before the next budget year begins and 18 months before the next budget year ends. In effect, educators from the classroom level up through the building level to the district level are being asked, in great detail, to determine their educational needs and priorities anywhere from 6 to 18 months in advance. Sometime after the first of the year these budget requests are submitted to the business office, they are consolidated, worked upon, a preliminary budget is developed and presented to the Board of Education and eventually the Board of Education either approves a budget or submits it for approval to either the voters of the school district or the governing body having oversight. This takes place sometime in late spring. Now obviously, the school district needs to have a budget, and the budget needs to have boundaries and a bottom line. But the devil, as always, is in the details demanded, which in many instances, is down to the individual purchase order level, vender, item description, and quantity. While this makes sense when considering the amount of copy paper, heating oil, and gasoline required for bidding, it does not make sense when deciding on the specifics of instructional materials, staff development, conference participation, and other variables that need to remain sufficiently flexible to allow for the dynamic world in which schools are now required to function. Pools of funds should be established to cover such anticipated expenditures. Where specific instructional expenses are known, of course they can be specified within the budget. But decisions to specify should not be forced because of budget development deadlines! Perhaps this will require the rethinking of some Superintendents, Business Managers, and members of Boards. Perhaps, thankfully, this transition has already begun in some districts. To fully allow the school improvement process to move to a dynamic mode, the budget process must follow suit. This is but one example of a process that needs to "flex" in order to allow planning to become dynamic.

As a cautionary step, perhaps it is wise to pause at this point and clarify the word "dynamic"." Dynamic comes to us through the French from the Greek as an adjective that meant "powerful" and/or "changeable"." It is used in English today in many fields ranging from physics to music. We learn much from its synonyms, which are: "active," "fluid," "moving," "energetic," and "powerful." We also learn much from its antonym which is: "static." I came to use the phrase dynamic planning because I wanted to describe a planning process that was active, fluid, moving, energetic, and powerful. A planning process that was continuous, never ending, nonstatic. I wanted a phrase that matched the world in which schools now find themselves.

Dynamic planning is based upon the following needs:

+ The need to focus on key student learning indicators (results)

+ The need for a process that becomes the way *"school"* does its business

+ The need for a process that is active, fluid, moving, and can quickly adjust to rapid change

+ The need to use data to identify problems and their root causes

+ The need to base decisions upon data rather than uninformed opinion

+ The need to enable wide-spread involvement in the process of change

+ The need to focus on key student learning indicators (a deliberate repetition)

The dynamic planning process can be initiated at any level within the school district but it functions best when it becomes the operational model for the whole of the district and has as its champion the superintendent of schools. The superintendent must model the process, integrate it into the fabric of school operations, and allow others to learn it through training and experience. This is the embodiment of the cliché: "walking the talk"." As superintendent, I met monthly with the principals and directors of the school district. The Dynamic Plan would provide the basis for each meeting agenda. It would be monitored and adjusted as needed. As superintendent, I met in public session with the board of education twice each month. Again, the Dynamic Plan would be a part of each agenda and they would be kept informed of changes, new data, and any other items of interest. As high school principal I met monthly with department chairs. Again the Dynamic Plan would form the basis for each meeting's agenda. Each of these meetings provides a platform for monitoring the implementation of the plan, evaluating its results and making modifications based upon the needs of the moment. Modifications can be made quickly and communicated via a series of updates to all impacted by the process. Dynamic planning is planning in motion.

The primary elements of dynamic planning are found in the definition below:

> *Dynamic planning* is an inclusive, continuous, databased process that creates linkages among all other school system processes, focuses them on improvement of key indicators of student success, and becomes the primary agenda by which the school system organizes its work.

Let's take a look at these elements of dynamic planning one at a time.

Inclusiveness: the dynamic planning process should be open, transparent, and include representatives of those who are expected to carry out the plan as well as representatives of those who will be impacted by the planning. Dynamic planning will most often include more than one level of planning, such as district, building, grade and/or program levels. Each level of planning, however, must support the system's overall learning goals. All members of the system must be aware of the planning process and have easy access to it. In another sense, Dynamic Planning must include planning for the major instructional and operational processes of the system. The Dynamic Plan must be sufficiently comprehensive to embrace all processes necessary for the achievement of the key indicators of student success. Inclusiveness requires open multidirectional communication.

Continuous: the dynamic planning process is ongoing and is never "complete". It always remains in motion, a work in progress. It is always an open process of communication throughout the system. It does not end and it does not become "shelf art"." It ignores, where it can, the traditional agrarian annual cycle of today's public education. It is too dynamic a process to be confined on a calendar that calls for revisions every twelve months. I am reminded of a facilitator who was once asked to share her plan with another work group. Her reply was along the lines of "I can't, it isn't done yet." Dynamic planning is never done! It remains pliable and open as additional needs of students emerge and as the wisdom of the school increases.

Databased: the dynamic planning process consumes data and transforms data into information, information into knowledge, knowledge into understanding, and understanding into wisdom. The best data-driven decisions are made at the level of understanding and wisdom. Data is used to identify problem areas. It is then used again and transformed to seek root cause. It is used again to evaluate progress and improvement. Types of data include: student achievement and progress data, school process data, demographic data, and perceptive data. It is data about students, the system, benchmarking data, and data regarding assessments. Dynamic planning is a data rich process and is a direct outgrowth of DBDM. It is focused DBDM in motion. Dynamic planning provides the framework that enables the linkages among myriad DBDM processes within the district.

Linkages: the dynamic planning process is strengthened when the central office, board, buildings, programs, departments, and grade levels have a common guiding vision of what is to be accomplished and how to work together to achieve it. Dynamic Planning must ultimately be linked to budget, to staffing, to recruitment, to staff development, to supervision and evaluation, to school improvement teams, to the Board of Education, to parents and to the community at large. Linkages require open multidirectional communication. Linkages help bring about alignment and focus upon achievement of the KISS.

School System: Your organization must be seen as a system with parts that interrelate and are aligned. As noted under the linkages element of dynamic planning, no part of the system is in isolation from other parts, even if it wants to be. See Chapter 5 on Systems. Site-based teams, program teams, district teams, all function on their parts of the system to ensure that individual students and cohorts are enabled to meet standards and the KISS.

Focus: the dynamic planning process aligns school district resources upon the attainment of specific levels of student proficiency and progress.

Key Indicators of Student Success: the dynamic planning process is built upon the identification and monitoring of KISS. These are key areas of skill, knowledge, and dispositions that all students are required to have before they can continue as active independent learners. These key indicators become the basis for initial data collection, and gap and root cause analysis. Both proficiency and progress are monitored.

The Primary Agenda: the dynamic planning process becomes the first point of reference or "guiding rail" for the daily work of the school. Because dynamic planning is continuous it can remain flexible and quickly responsive to needs for change. As "the agenda" it integrates the many functions of the school district toward the achievement of identified KISS and replaces or enhances previous management processes. Dynamic planning is not an "add-on extra" function. It is "the function"."

Some school districts, and perhaps many educators, have become inured to the "flavor of the week" syndrome due to over acceptance of whatever the carousel of educational fads has delivered to them over time. In such contexts it is best never to use the term "dynamic planning"." Proper implementation can be achieved simply by modifying present practice while slowly introducing the elements, vocabulary, and concepts. "That which we call a rose, by any other name would smell as sweet" (William Shakespeare). In fact, when dynamic planning becomes truly and fully implemented, it should become invisible as a "program" as it has long since simply become the way the district conducts its work.

While the most immediate, and perhaps primary, use of Dynamic Planning will be to focus the school's resources on areas of deficiency in KISS, dynamic planning can be, and should be, easily implemented within other school processes, such as, transportation, food services, budgeting, personnel, custodial and maintenance services. Indeed many of these same so-called "noninstructional" processes should be directly linked to the focus on student learning or support a positive learning environment in their own right. Likewise Key Indicators of Success can be identified for each of these processes, and then measured and analyzed. The school district must be seen as a system with all of its many parts and processes each contributing to the goal of improved student learning.

Dynamic Planning: Elements for Implementation

There are various elements required of successful implementation of dynamic planning. I originally organized them into steps, but steps are sequential and these elements are not necessarily sequential. The best that I can offer is that these elements are roughly organized into at least several stages, the adoption stage, implementation stage, expansion stage and then, hopefully, something called the optimizing stage. Let's take a look at each of these.

The Adoption Stage

It is during the *adoption stage* that the following items are either identified as being present or as in need of being present and then developed:

- ◆ Leadership* commitment to continuous improvement and change
- ◆ Sufficient leadership knowledge regarding dynamic planning in order to determine its potential
- ◆ Leadership commitment to implementation of dynamic planning as the tool for school operations and improvement
- ◆ Leadership awareness and understanding of key concepts

    Seeing the whole of the school district as a single system

    Providing initial dynamic planning staff development as necessary

    Identification of key indictors of student success

    Identification of or developing of data resources (data infrastructure)

- ◆ Develop an implementation plan
    - • Assign responsibilities to specific leaders
    - • Assign specific resources (clerical, time, financial, space, etc.)
    - • Assign timelines
    - • Identify anticipated results in terms of change

    *Leadership includes Superintendent, Board, and all instructional leaders, including business manager.

The Implementation Stage

During the implementation stage the following activities will be taking place, but not necessarily in this order.

- ◆ Implement the implementation plan.
- ◆ Monitor and evaluate the implementation plan.
- ◆ Begin the process of integrating dynamic planning into the daily work of the school by integrating dynamic planning into the agendas of the primary work groups of the school: the Board, cabinets, building teams, school improvement teams.
- ◆ Pick the low fruit first, beginning with one project per group, or more, as groups can handle.

♦ Move the whole school improvement process over to dynamic planning.

♦ Grow the infrastructure.

  • Improve team skills via staff development.

  • Improve whole staff skills and understanding via staff development and engagement.

  • Expand data resources via augmentation as needed.

  • Benchmark: learn what others are doing.

  • Attend conferences: getting outside your box.

  • Research the Internet.

These continuous improvement efforts take place during the implementation stage, and later during the expansion and optimization stages, the basic cycle follows very similar lines that are outlined below:

♦ Gather data measuring the KISS.

♦ Conduct gap analysis.

♦ Seek root cause for the largest and most immediate gaps in learning.

♦ Implement interventions (strategies) to dissolve the root causes.

♦ Monitor the implementation process. (Are we doing what we said we would do?)

♦ Evaluate results by gathering data, conduct gap analysis, etc. (Are we getting the results we expected? Wanted? Need?)

♦ Repeats the cycle.

The Expansion Stage

It is during this stage that the utilization of dynamic planning broadens across the school district into other departments and programmatic areas and gradually becomes more of an operational norm. Other school processes slowly adjust to the dynamic nature of dynamic planning and infrastructure develops to meet the rapidly growing demands for data and the analysis of data on other than annual or quarterly schedules. School leadership and all staff become more comfortable with the vocabulary and usage of data and of dynamic planning. DBDM becomes the norm. Linkages among DBDM teams are strengthened and decisions in isolation are becoming less frequent. Information begins to flow throughout the system. Barriers among and between programs, buildings, processes, and functions becomes lower. Focus on KISS increases. The system becomes more responsive.

The Optimizing Stage

What is this optimizing stage? It certainly is not an end point. In the context of continuous improvement there is no end point. It certainly cannot then be a point where the school district "has arrived"." What is it then? It is the point where dynamic planning and DBDM have become such an integral part of the the school district that they are the only way the school goes about its work. The transition from more or less static annual plans or worse has been made. The transition from long-range budget projections and hard-wired purchase orders to more flexibility in how monies can be spent has been made. Decisions without data, information, knowledge, understanding, and wisdom have nearly ceased. Real-time monitoring of student achievement and progress has been implemented. Real-time monitoring and adjustments are made. Student learning is improving. The school district is more successful at its primary task. The district is: active, fluid, moving, energetic, powerful, and non-static. The district has become dynamic. It is at this point that it must continue to fine tune, continue to learn, move on to the ever higher fruit, address the problems that have been the hardest to solve, and move on to the next level of skill, understanding, and wisdom.

The fundamental importance of internal system-wide communications cannot be over stressed. In the paragraphs above terms such as "open," "integrate," "include," "inclusive," "aware," and "align" have been used. All imply communication and none can be achieved without it. There are at least two large areas of knowledge that must be communicated and that must be known. The first is knowledge of the learning standards required of students, methods of assessing them, and the means by which they are best taught and learned. Proper instruction cannot take place without this knowledge and the skill to develop and incorporate tasks parallel to the standards and parallel to the way in which they will be assessed. Of course, this also requires the foundation of subject matter knowledge and skills along with the foundation of knowledge and skills regarding the instruction of youth. A label for this complex network of communications regarding instructional understandings could be "Pedagogical Content Knowledge"."

The second area of knowledge that must be constantly communicated is that regarding the inner workings of the system with regard to its processing of its dynamic plan. In other words:

♦ What is it doing to accomplish its goals in regard to meeting its KISS;

♦ How is it keeping to its schedule?

♦ What have been the results?

A label for this type of communication could be *"System Process Knowledge."*

One method of keeping constituents informed is through a process called "verification"." After every meeting where an action has been taken on part of any *"plan,"* a simple single-page update is sent to all constituents of that part of the process informing them of what was done and asking their input with questions such as, What did we miss? What did we do that was wrong? What other comments do you have? Any feedback is then used as part of the starting point for the next meeting of the group that initiated it. The term "constituents" includes any and all who may be expected to become involved in that part of the plan or who may be impacted by that part of the plan. In smaller districts it is conceivable that this might involve everyone, while in larger districts the feedback group would be much more restricted in nature.

Staff within any unit of the district should know and understand the district's basic goals and the unit they are in, the specific building and unit goals that are being worked upon at the present time, and the strategies that are being implemented to achieve those goals. Additionally, they should be aware of the structures in place that are working on these issues and with whom to share their concerns, questions, information, or suggestions.

Some years ago I was deeply involved in the piloting of the Comprehensive District Education Planning (CDEP) process in New York. After several days of reading completed plans submitted to the state for approval I came to the conclusion that there were two essential elements that must converge to enable the development of a successful plan. These two elements were the district's *commitment* to using the planning process as a tool for school improvement and the district's *capacity* to properly master the required skills and concepts. I felt at the time that these two elements were also interactive in that high commitment engendered greater capacity. In the reading of many CDEP plans I came to see that both commitment to the process and the capacity to carry it out became visible in the quality of the product. At the time I developed what I called the "District Commitment/Capacity Scale" as my attempt to capture what I saw as the components of both commitment and capacity and to place them into a rubric that could be used as a rough scale. In reviewing this chapter I came to realize that this same concept could apply to the implementation of Dynamic Planning and so I have slightly modified the Scale to conform to the vocabulary used in this text and have placed it in the Appendices in the hope that it might be of use to those who are serious about self-examination for the purpose of continuous improvement. My belief is that the ultimate success of Dynamic Planning rests upon the degree of district commitment and organizational capacity established in support of its implementation.

Summary

In this chapter I have introduced the concept and rationale for Dynamic Planning, provided and explained the elements of its definition, and discussed a sequence of four stages through which the application of Dynamic Planning within a school District may pass. The issue of communication has been discussed and two important types of communication identified: "Pedagogical Content Knowledge" and "System Process Knowledge." The concept of the District Commitment/Capacity Scale was introduced. In Chapter 6 we discuss issues involved with "making it happen."

Questions to Think About

1. How important is the planning process to you right now?
2. Would Dynamic Planning make any difference?
3. What would be the benefits to Dynamic Planning for you? For your system?
4. What would you see as the negative side of Dynamic Planning for you? For your system?
5. In what quadrant is your district's Commitment/Capacity?

    Quadrant 1   Low Commitment / Low Capacity

    Quadrant 2   Low Commitment / High Capacity

    Quadrant 3   High Commitment / Low Capacity

    Quadrant 4   High Commitment / High Capacity

7

Making It Happen

Making it happen is the crucial step in all processes of change and yet it is the step most fraught with danger. While all that has gone before in terms of planning and preparation are critical and necessary, it is at the point of "making it happen" that all of the various pieces have to be orchestrated together in such a way as to enable the vision to become a reality, a new system of doing school.

In thinking about this chapter two expressions that I often heard from my mother came to mind. The first, usually just before or during a very large task: "Rome wasn't built in a day." The second, typically as we traveled north on our way from New York City to Vermont in our Hudson Terraplane: "Great Caesar in all his glory never traveled like this." I believe both expressions aptly apply to the process of getting started with using data, databased decision making (DBDM), and dynamic planning.

"Rome wasn't built in a day." Some schools have a 10-year history of implementation of DBDM and have the infrastructure to support fairly sophisticated data-analysis processes and planning. While some schools are just starting out it will not take them as many years to develop to the same level. The late adopters have the advantage by learning from the mistakes and successes of the early adopters. Late adopters can "benchmark" the best practices of the early adopters and save years in their own learning curve. In some shape or form, all schools will ultimately have to develop the necessary infrastructure and this will enable all schools to make full use of the power of DBDM and dynamic planning.

Some years ago Mark Scharenbroich, (http://www.marktheteacher.com/) an inspirational, award winning, motivational speaker, presented a full day's program of assemblies at our high school. His presentations were nothing short of fantastic and I still have a copy of his "I am Creed" today. During one of the assemblies he asked a girl to come up to the stage and then asked her if she could lift one hundred pounds over her head. She shook her head "no," simultaneously partially embarrassed at being on stage and loving every moment of it. Mark then took one of our 10-pound rigging weights out from behind the curtain and asked her if she could lift the 10 pounds over her head 10 times. She nodded "yes." Mark's point was that tasks that appeared to be impossible become possible when they are broken down into smaller pieces. That is exactly the sentiment behind "Rome wasn't built in a day" and the concepts found within this chapter on "making it happen" with DBDM and dynamic planning. We can start with 10-pound weights and build from there.

"Great Caesar in all his glory never traveled like this." Never before in human history have we had such ready access to data or the ability to make use of it. Never before have we possessed the machines that could process hours of human computations in seconds or less. Never before have we developed the intelligence necessary to construct integrated data systems to inform our decisions and actions. Great Caesar never had a laptop, desktop, or blackberry. What we can accomplish with computerized data is nearly unreal. We are at the cusp of learning how to maximize its work on behalf of improved student learning. This relatively newfound ability also brings with it the expectation that it will be used and that through its use improved student learning will, indeed, occur.

Component Tasks Leading to the Data Revolution

What are the small "10-pound" tasks that need to be accomplished in order to make a data revolution in our school happen? The relative importance of the tasks on this list will vary depending upon which state you work in. Some state education departments have taken the lead in assisting state-wide efforts to implement DBDM, others only in some random ways and still others not at all. The relative importance will also vary based upon the context of the school district. Neighboring districts within the same state may have vastly different circumstances when it comes to the ability to use data. The list has many components and is not necessarily sequential although I have made an attempt at making it flow logically. In fact, a number of these activities can be occurring simultaneously. In all honesty, some of the tasks may be closer to 5 pounds while others are nearly 20.

1. Identify key indicators of student success. (KISS)
2. Identify what measures will be used to assess KISS.
3. Conduct a data inventory within the school listing all types of data currently available.
4. Note the format in which the data is kept, its availability, and its "gate keeper."
5. Identify what additional data is needed in order to measure KISS.
6. Develop a plan to obtain the additional data (this may take time).
7. Make use of the data in assessing each KISS.

   Conduct a gap analysis. Where are we? Where do we want to be?

   Conduct root cause analysis (RCA) on the most significant gaps.

8. Select remedies, interventions, strategies, to dissolve the root cause(s).

9. Develop an implementation plan and schedule and assign responsibility.

10. Develop a monitoring plan. Are we doing what we said we would do?

11. Develop an evaluation plan. Are we making a difference in the outcome?

12. Continue the process.

Remember to make these items *transparent* (Chapter 6, p. 83).

Let's review these twelve tasks. Staff development is a crucial issue in many of these steps above.

In task 1, staff must be able to understand the concept of "key indicator of student success" and the importance of getting this item right because it becomes the basis for all that follows. Likewise with measurement tools, some things cannot be measured directly, but can be assumed by the measurement of something that is measureable. Today, in astronomy, there is a massive search for planets outside of our Solar System. These planets most times cannot be seen but are inferred from the wobble of their home star. In the nearby tourist village of Lake George in New York State, summer visitor levels are partially measured by parking meter returns and sewerage flows. It may not be possible to directly measure "student engagement" with their school, so a proxy measurement must be found. In one district the staff felt that participation in activities outside of the classroom could be used as such a measure. In another district a student survey was administered that attempted to measure student engagement among several other issues.

While working with one school district the Superintendent became frustrated that the district team (composed of staff, students, parents and community members) had taken nearly three years and still had not finalized a set of key indicators—he threatened to come up with a set of his own and indeed had a set in reserve to use. The team arrived at a set of key indicators but did not believe that they would indeed be used to "drive the system." As they saw the KISS take hold and begin to drive the system they then began to question what they had developed. It was an interesting process to both participate in and reflect upon.

At this point in history, many school districts can simply start with the KISS already being demanded of them by their states and NCLB. If they find that they are already far beyond meeting these requirements, then they should move on to the next step of identifying what additional KISS are important within their own context. This process should involve more than just staff and should include Board, parent, and community as well. Many districts already have established a process to facilitate such inclusion.

Staff development perhaps is best given at the point where the training is to be applied. I think it is most beneficial when training can be merged with application and a workable product emerges from the staff-development session or sessions. It is at these times that the theoretical becomes practical. The question arises regarding obtaining human resources to conduct the staff development. In larger districts there are perhaps internal resources that can be used. In smaller and middle-sized districts there are BOCES or intermediate units that offer services. There are also independent consultants, universities, and larger consulting organizations. In the context of this chapter, the content is well defined and the district will want to ensure that the delivery of the training matches the expectations and needs that it has identified.

Tasks 3, 4, and 5 should be handled administratively with a minimum of staff time devoted to it except to review the information when it is presented and suggest additions, corrections, and deletions.

Task 6 items are crucial and must be completed by the staff working on the issue. Staff development in the areas of concept and process will most certainly be required before root cause analysis (RCA) can be accomplished and even a basic understanding of gap analysis might need to be strengthened.

Task 7 is yet another crucial step as the remedies must be aimed at the identified root cause(s) and not at the symptoms. Care must be taken to ensure that the selected remedies are in keeping with the core values and beliefs of the system.

Implementation planning and scheduling of task 8, have been found, in my experience, to be one of the major snags. Educators are not typically trained or called upon to think of or make use of project planning. While serving as high school principal I experienced three building projects. Once every week I sat in on the project planning session. In attendance were: the architect, project manager or clerk of the works, high school principal, superintendent of schools, and managers from each of the three major contractors. Once every week this team reviewed the progress of the plan to date, flagging things that were behind and flagging, in anticipation, things that would become delayed. An updated project calendar was developed before the conclusion of the meeting. Each person had a chance to express their needs or concerns and the plan was modified accordingly. Very little was written down except for notes. Before the group broke up there was a common understanding of what would take place over the next five days of work. Then there would be another meeting to update the plan. This is a great example of dynamic planning in action. It is essential that DBDM have an implementation plan and that the plan be dynamic and kept green. Individuals who are responsible need to be identified and held accountable for their responsibilities. An old Finnish proverb teaches that "Well planned is half done." It is our old concept of a static plan that needs to be demolished.

Tasks 9, 10, and 11: The implementation plan needs to be constantly monitored to ensure that it is being carried out on schedule and that the various steps are being taken. If not, adjustments need to be made and communicated. The end result, or goal, of the intervention needs to be evaluated. Are we making a difference? If not, why not? If yes, we are making a difference, does that mean the intervention is working or are other factors at work? Can we move on to other issues? Task 11, the process never ends—it is continuous and ongoing. It is the way the school goes about its most important business, the instruction that leads to learning. There is always work to be done. Improvement is continuous.

Let's continue with our listing starting with task 13 below:

13	Develop a method by which data can be digitally stored and queried. Pick a means of establishing a "data warehouse."
14	Identify what data elements will be stored in the data warehouse.
15	Establish data standards and requirements.
16	Identify and bring on board technical assistance and statistical assistance.
17	Identify the school's Chief Information Officer (CIO).
18	Develop a process whereby the data warehouse is easily accessible to teachers, administrators and other staff.

Task 13, develop a method by which data can be digitally stored and queried. Pick a means of establishing a *data warehouse*. There are a great variety of products available on the market to meet this need. The trick is to properly research each and to select the product that most closely approximates your present and future needs and pocketbook. Where states have already established a universal student data-repository system your choices may be more limited because the product you select will have to interact with the state system. A major consideration from my experience, is ease of use. If the warehouse is not intuitive, and if it requires many hours of staff training or practice before it can be used, its value for DBDM and dynamic planning will decrease exponentially. I have experienced this first hand, in both directions, my attempt to make use of what I thought to be a difficult to use system and my success in working with what I thought was a very easy to use system. No matter the system, training will be required. But stand guard against those systems that will eat up the resources of time and good will before they can become implemented. If you are working with an outside agency or contracting organization such as Battelle for Kids you will no doubt have solid assistance based upon experience in making your decision. It is wise, as well, to check into schools that have already embarked upon data warehousing, learn from their mistakes and successes.

Task 14, identify what data elements will be stored in the data warehouse. This is not a simple task. Hopefully data elements will reflect requirements for the monitoring of KISS as well as the desire to disaggregate student data by certain specific variables. An example of a "currently in use" model is found in New York State (NYS) at the URL listed at the end of this paragraph. This is part of the NYS Student Information Repository System, a state-wide system for the gathering and collecting of student data. The Dictionary of Reporting Data Elements is over 100 pages in length and provides a detailed view of what a state system looks like. The dictionary contains 5 sections (Athrough E) with approximately 67-individual data fields for each student. I could see the necessity of expanding the number of data fields considerably if one were to include such items as teacher-given grades while also attempting to maintain longitudinal information. Again, remember the adage: "pick the low fruit first." I doubt that it is at all possible, or desirable to initiate the construction of a data warehouse with the purpose of having it all done at one time. Of course the initial pattern of how it is organized will dictate future flexibility, so it is wise to establish it in such a way that it can be expanded far beyond its starting size. One can easily be overwhelmed by the amount of data that schools generate on an annual basis. The trick is to identify those data elements that are most salient to the initial steps being taken into DBDM and dynamic planning. I have given some examples of data elements in earlier chapters on data and data pathways. New York State's website on its "Student Information Repository System" is http://www.emsc.nysed.gov/irts/SIRS/documentation/DataDictionary.doc

Task 15, establish data standards and requirements. This also is often not an easy task. Feeding data from previously separate data systems into a single data warehouse causes all sorts of problems. For example, is Bobby Smith the same student as Robert J. Smith? Frequently separate data systems had no standard for entering data, each using data standards that worked for them while they remained in their silo. But now that the silos are being destroyed and we are seeking to combine student data from across the system we need uniform standards for data fields. Another problem that has occurred frequently is the crippling effect of incorrect data. Because data was so seldom used it did not often matter if it was correct. Now that it is being used, and it is being used in conjunction with other data sets that are equally flawed, the problem of cleansing data, in itself, becomes a large task. Hopefully, once the initial period of data reorganization and cleansing takes place and after uniform standards and element requirements are established, the problem will slowly melt away and remembered only as a start-up migraine.

Task 16, identify and bring on board technical assistance and statistical assistance. If it has not already occurred to you, let me just state that tasks 12 to 14 above need the assistance of a technical advisor and a statistician. Principals and superintendents, or their assistants, should not be expected to do these things on their own. They already have fulltime tasks to perform. Rarely do they have the full tool box of necessary skills. Principals, superintendents, and their assistants are leaders in their own right and need to be leading the implementation charge, but with the advice of those who are technically and statistically skilled. It says a lot when the chief administrator is at the table and takes part in the training. Likewise it says a lot when they don't. Why both technical and statistical assistance? First of all, the technical person knows how to set up the warehouse and how to make it work. I have found, however, that the technician's limitation is in knowing what is necessary for the warehouse to produce. In some cases the technician just dumped a lot of data on sheets for staff to utilize, not realizing that the data dump was not what was needed. Here is where the statistician, or more commonly used, the data analyst, comes in. The statistician/data analyst is the bridge between the technician and the educator. This person knows what is needed in a professionally and statistically meaningful way and is able to communicate that to the technician. The data analyst keeps administrators and staff from making statistical errors that are usually taught in Statistics 101 and 102. Perhaps it is analogous to the partnership between the bus driver and the tour director. The driver is certainly a skilled individual who knows how to make the bus run and how to squeeze it into and through tight spaces. The tour director, however, knows where the bus has to go and what the passengers expect to see. Having a skilled and friendly bus driver certainly adds to passenger enjoyment, but even more so when the tour director is able to produce how the tour was advertised. The Superintendent, or other key educational leader, is the "tour director" and is in charge of getting the team to where it has to go and to where they expect to be. The data analyst is the "driver" who has the technical skill to ensure that the vehicle being used (the data) is used properly and in such a way that the team indeed arrives at its destination safely.

I need to go just a bit more deeply into this topic. Schools, for many good reasons, have staff in the form of account clerks that assist the business manager in dealing with the myriad financial details of the district. This is all proper and good. But until very recently few if any school districts had an equivalent staff to account for student learning. I ask "What business are we in!" We are in the business of enabling learning. Yes we need to count pennies, but we need to measure progress and proficiency for each child as well. Slowly the light is dawning across the nation and an ever increasing number of districts are establishing dedicated staff for this purpose.

A word about outsourcing this process: Many school districts are too small to afford their very own technician and statistician/data analyst. They must seek ways of sharing such resources with other smaller districts either through such agencies as a BOCES or through commercial ventures that will function in these capacities. In doing outsourcing, however, it is essential that the people working with the school function and appear as though they are indeed essential members of the staff.

Task 17, identify the school's Chief Information Officer (CIO). Every school should have someone in charge of the school's data and informational resources. This position should be the point position for all that has been identified above. This function should report directly to the superintendent, or building principal (as the case may be), and the technicians and data analysts should report to the CIO. The CIO should play a helpful role in tasks 1 through 12 and a directing role in tasks 13 through 18

Task 18, develop a process whereby the data warehouse is easily accessible to teachers, administrators, and other staff. This relates back to task 13. Not only should the warehouse be intuitive and easy to learn, it must also be proximate—perhaps available at the teachers or administrator's desk and available from home via identifier and password. Coincident with the issue of accessibility is the degree to which the CIO and/or the data analyst can respond directly to administrative, committee, and individual requests for data to be queried in a specific manner. At the beginning of the data revolution in education a consultant from England made a compelling argument for why teachers and administrators should not be expected to conduct their own analysis, but rather they should be able to make requests for analysis. Committees and teams should not do the analysis but rather should respond to the analysis and make decisions based upon it. His argument included the fact that teachers and administrators already had a fulltime job. He went on to share that most administrators and teachers remembered little of Statistics 101 and 102 and probably would not be very good at analysis. He illustrated that point by giving his audience a relatively simple verbal mathematical problem. After a few minutes he asked for answers. They were multiple and varied, proving that at least this group of educators assembled before him were not the most agile in conducting analysis, even at the level of this simple problem. In the real world, however, administrators and teachers are often called upon, and are willing to undertake, extensive work beyond their normal work load if there is resulting benefit to them and their students. It might take just this sort of effort to start the wheel of DBDM and dynamic planning turning, but to keep it turning will require greater resources in terms of personnel, training, and accessibility.

EnGauge, a new Web-based framework developed by the North Central Regional Educational Laboratory (NCREL) is located at the URL listed below and contains foundational information regarding the correct implementation and use of data-driven decision making (D3M) within schools. The separate web pages focus on: Practice, Rationale, Roles, Links, Continuum, and References. They have also developed a rubric consisting of six essential conditions for effective use of technology. The essential conditions are: Vision, Educator Proficiency, Systems and Leadership, Equity, Effective Practice, and Access. The web pages are well worth reading as food for thought during the process of getting started.

♦ URL for framework items: http://www.ncrel.org/engauge/ framewk/sys/data/sysdatin.htm

♦ URL for framework rubric: http://www.ncrel.org/engauge/ framewk/index.htm

So, have I buried the concept of making it happen with an overload of 18 tasks that no single person in her right mind would seek to undertake? Perhaps so, but hopefully not. The process can begin with focus upon a single KISS and several sets of data regarding it, no data warehouse, no technician, no statistician/data analyst—just the folks around the table and a desire to improve student learning in the area of this one key indicator. But it cannot stop at this level in today's urgent climate of accountability and demand for learning. It must grow into a system-wide process of measuring key performance outcomes and the progress of students over time. And so we return to the concept that "Rome wasn't built in a day" and that "Caesar in all his glory" never had a data warehouse like ours. It takes many 10-pound lifts to successfully lift 100 pounds and so it is with the implementation of DBDM and dynamic planning. The goal, however, should always be to lift the 100 pounds, to develop the data warehouse, and to make maximal use of its contents for decision making and dynamic planning.

I would encourage those leading and participating in DBDM and dynamic planning transformational efforts of their system to engage in reading, not only of texts such as this and other educational articles and books, some of which I have listed in the Bibliography, but also texts such as those few listed in the "Parallel Readings Bibliography" from other realms that I believe provide a meaningful message for today's educational leaders.

Summary

In this chapter I have reviewed 18-fundamental tasks that are required for a school system to maximize their potential for both DBDM and dynamic planning. Although the tasks seem large, they need not be all done at once, nor is it required that any one of the 18 be done in one leap. The magic is to commit to starting the process and to maintain focus as the process of transformation unfolds. Rome was not built in a day and neither will the infrastructure necessary for sophisticated DBDM and dynamic planning. Never in human history have we had the tools available such as we have today. Commitment to, focus upon, and perseverance to complete the 18 tasks will win at the end of the day and will assist the reader in "making it happen."

Questions to Think About

1. At what stage is the development of my (our) system's data "infra-structure"?

    ☐ Haven't started yet

    ☐ Beginning

    ☐ Intermediate

    ☐ Advanced

2. If less than advanced, what is needed to get my system to the next step?

3. Have I (we) benchmarked my (our) infrastructure against those who are further advanced than we are? If so, what have we learned? If not, why not?

4. Do I (we) have a plan in place to develop our data infrastructure?

    If not, why not?

    If so, is it on schedule? If not, why not?

    If it is on schedule, are we getting the results we need, want, expected?

5. Is our planning beginning to become dynamic or is it still annual?

Glossary

The Glossary offers the definition of terms as they are used in this text. Its most important use is as a resource in developing a common vocabulary and *understanding of the terms* among all staff engaged in school improvement efforts. Without a common vocabulary, and without common knowledge of the terms, we can often assume agreement and understanding where there is none.

Action Plan Also called an "implementation plan." The action plan is the product of a root cause analysis process that identifies the strategies to be implemented to dissolve the root cause, who is going to do what, on what schedule and with what resources, to implement each strategy.

Action Planning The process of creating an action or implementation plan.

Akrasia A Greek word meaning "weakness of will." More recently used to describe the action people take to engage in high-risk behavior when much safer alternatives are available. In this text, *akratic behavior* is making school decisions without the use of data.

Barrier Analysis A Root Cause Analysis process whereby barriers to improvement are identified, verified, and removed as well as necessary, barriers to failure are identified, verified, and implemented.

Benchmarking A process by which a school district compares the measures of its key indicators with those of several similar districts to determine how well it is doing in comparison to others. If other districts are achieving better results, a benchmarking visit or consultation is in order to learn how the better results have been achieved. Benchmarking may also take place in comparison to the same school district over time and in comparison to state or national standards.

CDEP Comprehensive District Educational Planning: a process piloted and adopted by over 150-school districts in New York State beginning in 1997 and continuing through 2002 (although many districts continue to use CDEP).

Cohort Used to describe a single assemblage of students, frequently a whole grade level, such as, an entering ninth-grade cohort or a similar larger group.

Common Cause Variation Variation within a process that is a normal part of the process.

Control   A process is said to be in control when special cause variation is eliminated and only common cause variation is present. In this state the output of the process can be predicted within certain specified limits.

Control Chart   Used in statistical process control (SPC) to show the output of a process over time, and when computed, the upper and lower control limits of the process—sometimes called a run chart.

Control Limits   A derivative of standard deviation that shows the predictable upper and lower limits of a process's output. All variation within these control limits is considered normal. Variation either above or below the control limits is considered to be special cause variation.

Culture   School culture is a complex composite of history, values, assumptions, norms, and attitudes that manifest themselves in school climate and artifacts such as policies, procedures, methods, styles of communication, and processes. Cultural elements are often "latent" causes.

Creative Root Cause Analysis   A group RCA process taught at the Dow Leadership Development Center of Hillsdale College, Hillsdale, Michigan.

Databased Decision Making   DBDM is a system of deeply rooted beliefs, actions, and processes that infuses organizational culture and regularly organizes and transforms data to wisdom for the purpose of making organizational decisions

Data Pathway   As used in Chapter 3, a data pathway is a metaphor for the four possible investigative routes that should be taken in both converting data to information to knowledge to understanding to wisdom and in seeking root causes for both problems and successes. The four data pathways are: the student, system, benchmarking, and assessment pathways.

Data Pathway Lanes   As used in Chapter 3, each data pathway is composed of at least several lanes. Each of these pathway lanes is identified and explained in the chapter.

Dataset   Used to describe any collection of data that describes a relatively narrow set of outcomes, such as, attendance rates.

Data Warehousing   A system of storing large amounts of data electronically over time for the purpose of rapid retrieval and querying. An essential tool for examining large amounts of data in order to support databased decision making and dynamic planning.

Desired Ideal Condition   The condition we should all strive for, the perfect result, such as, 100% attendance or successful completion of a course, grade, or diploma requirements. It is often used as the target for school improvement efforts.

Diagnostic Tree   A root cause analysis tool that provides a guided structure for digging deeply to find cause. Main branches include: student demographics, curriculum, instruction, school processes, and school culture.

Disaggregation The process of taking basic, level-one data and breaking it apart into smaller components based upon identified key factors. Student test data, for example, may be broken down or disaggregated by age, gender, ethnicity, sending school, zip code, language spoken, etc.

Dynamic Planning   An inclusive, continuous, databased process that creates linkages among all other school system processes, focuses them on improvement of key indicators of student success, and becomes the primary agenda by which the school system organizes its work.

Ends Ends are the purpose of school, not the strategies, materials, methods, or other means of achieving them. Essential ends are most clearly stated as key indicators of student success.

Error Coding   A process whereby student-constructed responses on assessments are not only scored for correctness, but when less than perfect, are coded according to a uniform set of errors. Error coding provides detailed information about "why" students responded incorrectly.

EVAAS   A trademarked product of SAS, which is their analytic system for providing value-added services.

Evaluation   Is what we are doing (strategies for improvement) making a difference? If not, why not?

Fishbone Diagram A graphic tool that shows the relationship among the many causes of a problem. It is also called a cause and effect diagram or an Ishikawa diagram.

Five Whys, The A simple process used to seek root cause by asking "Why," five times in succession.

Flow Chart   A chart that graphically shows the flow of a process. Used as a tool to explain, verify, and communicate exactly how a process functions.

Force Field Analysis   A process whereby the driving and restraining forces acting on a system are identified and placed on a graphic for visual consideration. The theory indicates that the system will move in the desired direction wanted by removal, or decreasing, the restraining forces rather than only by building the driving forces, which will create increased pressure.

Frontier Analysis   A sophisticated statistical benchmarking process whereby a school district can identify similar schools that are performing at the "frontier" of expectations in terms of student achievement.

Gap   The difference between desired student performance outcomes and actual student achievement.

Gantt Chart   A horizontal bar chart developed by Henry Gantt in 1917 to assist in production control. With the addition of the identification of the party responsible for each element, it provides a useful means for monitoring implementation action plans and communicating what is to be accomplished when and by whom.

Goal Statement   A complete *ends*-focused goal statement must contain these elements: be focused on a key indicator (of student success), be a specific target (for achievement or progress) compared to the present, and be a time frame for achievement of the target.

Google   Google is the world's largest Internet search it receives and processes over 2.5 billion queries each day (Wikepedia). To "google" is to use this search engine to query the Internet for information regarding a specific topic. The company has expanded to include a broad range of other products and services.

Implementation Plan   Also called an "action plan," the implementation plan is the product of a root cause analysis process that identifies the strategies to be implemented to dissolve the root cause and who is going to do what ,on what schedule, and with what resources to implement each strategy.

Key Indicator   A selected measure of a school's success, which has been formally identified, publicly verified, and that is monitored as part of an ongoing school improvement planning process. Most typically they are student focused measurable outcomes that the school has the ability, desire, or need to influence and for which it is willing, or required, to be held accountable. These are called *key indicators of student success.*

Levels of Root Cause   Root causes can be found at ever deeper layers of the school. Levels include: the incident, program, whole system, and external causes.

Level One Data   The initial aggregated dataset, prior to disaggregation or further analysis. Used to identify "red flag" issues.

Level Two Data   A deeper data set, usually a disaggregation of an initial set of aggregated data. As Level Two Data is further disaggregated and analyzed it becomes Level Three Data and so on.

Link and Linkages   "Systems are not the sum of their parts but rather the product of their interactions." Links and linkages are the "things" that enable the parts of the system to interact in such a way as to meet the goals of the system. These "things" include open multi-directional communication, alignment, articulation, universal vision, leadership, and a variety of other ingredients that allow the parts of the system to interact freely.

Lower Control Limit   A computed number that indicates the predictable lower limit of a process's output. Any output below this limit is considered to be special cause variation and is an indication that the process is out of control.

Means The "things we do" in order to achieve our goals (ends). In schools this will include items such as methods and materials of instruction, curriculum, staff development, scheduling, budgeting, assessment, planning, communication, and special programs and processes.

Modalities of Root Cause Although root cause analysis is most frequently used in a negative reactive mode (looking back to find out why something went wrong), it can also be used in at least three other modalities. In the positive reactive mode one looks back to find out what went right. In the positive proactive mode one looks forward to learn what has to be in place for a new process to be successful. In the negative proactive mode one looks forward to learn what has to be dissolved for a new process to be successful.

Monitor Are we doing what we said we would do?

Multiple Measures of Data Dr. Victoria Bernhardt has provided this very useful model of the multiple types of data that are used in root cause analysis. They are: student achievement data, student demographic data, school system and process data, and stakeholder perception data. Often a single dataset, such as student grades, can be used both as a measure of student achievement and also of the school system and its processes.

Need Needs are gaps in student learning between where students should be and where they actually are.

P-Scores Simply the percentage of students in a sample that answered a specific multiple choice question correctly. Where P = 0.75, 75% of the students answered the item correctly. P-scores are used to determine item difficulty and the degree to which local students responded correctly as compared to a much larger regional cohort.

Paretoing A tool used in root cause analysis to "weight" through voting, the various factors identified as possible root causes. The pareto concept being that 80% of the result comes from the most important 20% of the factors (80% of class cuts come from 20% of the student body).

Patch A "solution" that deals only with the symptom or proximate cause rather than with the root cause. Patching results in increased cost and complexity and does not dissolve the problem.

Performance Goal A target for a specific level of student performance to be achieved with a specified time frame, usually tied to a key indicator of student performance and a specified measure, such as an assessment.

Problem A situation where performance does not meet expectation.

Process All work is process. Processes have three components: inputs, some sort of process or action, and an output. Once one can identify all three components, the full process can be defined. The term "process" also is used to define mini-systems nested within larger systems (instructional processes within the school system).

Questioning Data   A process used to seek root cause by "seeing" what data has to tell them and identifying "questions" about what is seen as a basis for further investigation. The questioning data process has two primary phases: Phase I consists of answering the question "What do I see in this data?" and Phase II consists of answering the question "What questions do I have about what I see in this data?". The process uses both individual and group process to arrive at group products to these questions.

Red-Flag Issue   Something in a dataset that causes the reader to assess that something significant is happening (or not happening) and that needs to be investigated further. It is usually an obvious discrepancy between expectation and result.

Root Cause   The deepest underlying cause or causes of positive or negative symptoms within any process, which if dissolved, would result in elimination or substantial reduction of the symptom.

SAS   A business intelligence and analysis company doing business with over 43,000 clients and having gross income in excess of $2 billion that has partnered with Dr. William Sanders and provides value-added analytical services to school districts via its EVAAS product.

Scattergram   A tool used to display the correlation or interaction of two variables on a chart. Also called a scatter diagram.

Special Cause Variation   Variation within a process that is not normal and is typically caused by some type of special event or circumstance.

Stable Process   A process that exhibits only common cause variation.

Standard   An agreed upon and established statement of expectations for students focused on issues of learning, attitude, and behavior. Standards drive key indicators of student success.

Statistical Process Control   The methods by which a process is measured to determine if its variation is normal or special cause.

Student Achievement   As measured by a standardized assessment, this indicates the level of proficiency a student has gained within a content area at a specific point in time.

Student Progress   As measured in a value-added system it indicates the growth in learning a student or cohort of students achieves over time.

Symptom   The most immediate visible sign of a problem (need).

System   A simple system consists of an input and a valued added activity, resulting in a defined and expected output. Complex systems consist of many such processes, linked together to form a complex outcome. Systems nest within systems (class, course, department, school, district).

Target A student performance goal that a school sets that should indicate a score (rate) and a timeline for reaching that score (rate).

Team A group that is dynamic and working together toward a well-defined goal. Implies greater linkages and engagement than a committee.

Timeline A tool used to graphically display a sequence of events.

Triangulation A process of gathering multiple datasets to focus in on understanding an issue rather than relying upon a single form of evidence. Multiple forms of data provide a more distinct and valid picture of reality.

Underlying Cause Those causes that contribute to the proximate cause.

Unstable Process A process that is "out of control" due to special cause variation.

Upper Control Limit A computed number that indicates the predictable upper limit of a process's output. Any output above this limit is considered to be special cause variation and is indication that the process is out of control.

Value-Added Analyses Value-added analysis is a statistical method used to measure the influence of a district and school on the academic progress rates of individual students and groups of students from year-to-year and which performs as a system of deeply rooted beliefs, actions, and processes that infuses organizational culture and regularly transforms data to wisdom for the purpose of making organizational decisions for the purpose of improving student learning.

Variation Differences in outcome over time.

> **Common Cause** Variation that is a natural part of each process and a consequence of the process itself.

> **Special Cause** Variation that is unique, and often a result of a special influencing factor, which causes the process to become unstable and out of control. Usually located outside of the process being examined or from the larger system of which it is a part.

Verification The process by which a team product is publicly disseminated and reviewed for the purpose of using the input generated to modify the product before it becomes finalized.

Acronyms

BOCES	Board of Cooperative Educational Services
CCSSO	The Council of Chief State School Officers
CIO	Chief Information Officer
CDEP	Comprehensive District Education Plan
DATAG	School Data Analysts Group
DBDM	Databased Decision Making
DP	Dynamic Planning
D3M	Data-Driven Decision Making
D3A2	Data Driven Decisions for Academic Achievement (Ohio)
ECS	The Education Commission of the States
EFF	Education for the Future: A California-based educational initiative led by Dr. Victoria Bernhardt
FAA	Federal Aviation Administration
KISS	Key Indicators of Student Success
McREL	Mid-Continent Research for Education and Learning
NCLB	No Child Left Behind
NCREL	North Central Regional Educational Laboratory
NSSE	National Study for School Evaluation
NYS	New York State
PDE	Pennsylvania Department of Education
PSSA	Pennsylvania System of School Assessment
PVAAS	Pennsylvania Value-Added Assessment System
RCA	Root Cause Analysis
SAS	Name of company that provides software and technology for value-added analysis and data-driven performance management. (no longer an acronym)
SCANS	Secretary's Commission on Achieving Necessary Skills
SPC	Statistical Process Control
TICAL	The Technology Information Center for Administrative Leadership
TVAAS	The Tennessee Value-Added Assessment System
URL	Uniform Resource Locator: simply the world wide Internet address of a specific resource. All locations on the Internet must have a URL.

VAA	Value-Added Analysis
VARC	Value-Added Research Center (located at WCER listed below)
WCER	Wisconsin-Madison Center for Educational Research (Madison)

Bibliographies

In keeping with the concept first expressed in the Introduction to this text the Bibliography has purposefully been kept brief as a means of focusing the reader upon those few resources with the greatest benefit (see Pareto in Glossary). Actually, the many Internet-based resources identified throughout the text should serve as primary jumping off points for those seeking additional information and the texts listed in the Bibliographies should serve as resources for those preparing themselves as trainers or first-line leaders of Dynamic Planning and Databased Decision Making implementation efforts.

Foundations Bibliography

The texts below are what I call foundational texts in that they have provided the basic information upon which much of my thinking and work is based. I suggest their use for those who truly want to establish a firm grasp of the fundamentals and for those whose function is to train others.

Brassard, Michael, (1996) *The Memory Jogger Plus+*, Methuen, MA; Goal/QPC (PB 306 pages, ISBN – 1-879364-83-2).

Deming, W. Edwards, (1982)*Out of the Crisis* Cambridge, MA; MIT Center for Advanced Engineering Study (HC 507 pages, ISBN – 0-911379-01-0).

Senge, Peter M., (1990) *The Fifth Discipline: The Art and Practice of the Learning Organization*, New York; Doubleday, (HC 424 pages, ISBN – 0-385-26094-6).

Tucker, Sue, (1996) *Benchmarking: A Guide for Educators* Thousand Oaks, CA; Corwin Press (PB 82 pages, ISBN – 0-8039-6367-X).

Wheeler, Donald J., (1993) *Understanding Variation: The Key to Managing Chaos*, Knoxville, TN; SPC Press, (HC 136 pages ISBN – 0-945320-35-3).

Because I have referenced my text on root cause analysis in Chapter 5 on Key Concepts, I thought it best to include it in this section of the Bibliography:

Preuss, Paul G., (2002) *A School Leader's Guide to Root Cause Analysis: Using Data to Dissolve Problems*, Larchmont, NY; Eye On Education (ISBN 1-930556-53-5).

Dr. Victoria Bernhardt Bibliography

As noted in Chapter 2, Dr. Bernhardt is a gifted author and presenter who has had significant impact across the nation on using data to bring about school improvement. Each of the texts below is filled with real-time examples and detailed information that provide clear direction for those wishing to improve learning for all students.

Using Data to Improve Student Learning in School Districts, Larchmont, NY; Eye On Education, (2006, ISBN 1-59667-029-0)
http://www.eyeoneducation.com/prodinfo.asp?number=7029%2D0

Using Data to Improve Student Learning in High Schools Larchmont, NY; Eye On Education, (2005, ISBN 1-59667-004-5)
http://www.eyeoneducation.com/prodinfo.asp?number=7004%2D5

Data Analysis for Continuous School Improvement, Larchmont, NY; Eye On Education, (2004, ISBN 1-930556-74-8)
http://www.eyeoneducation.com/prodinfo.asp?number=674%2D8

Using Data to Improve Student Learning in Middle Schools, Larchmont, NY; Eye On Education (2004, ISBN 1-59667-029-0)
http://www.eyeoneducation.com/prodinfo.asp?number=687%2DX

Using Data to Improve Student Learning in Elementary Schools Larchmont, NY; Eye On Education (2003, ISBN 1-930556-60-8)
http://www.eyeoneducation.com/prodinfo.asp?number=660%2D8

The School Portfolio Tool Kit, Larchmont, NY; Eye On Education, (2002, ISBN 1-930556-21-7)
http://www.eyeoneducation.com/prodinfo.asp?number=621%2D7

The Example School Portfolio, Larchmont, NY; Eye On Education (2000, ISBN 1-883001-92-7)
http://www.eyeoneducation.com/prodinfo.asp?number=092%2D7

Translating Data into Information to Improve Teaching and Learning, Larchmont, NY; Eye On Education (2007, ISBN 978-1-59667-061-7)
http://www.eyeoneducation.com/prodinfo.asp?number=7061%2D7

Dr. Bernhardt's texts contain her *School Continuous Improvement Continuums* that are rubrics covering five degrees of: approach, implementation, and outcome in each of the following areas:

- ♦ Information and Analysis
- ♦ Student Achievement
- ♦ Quality Planning
- ♦ Professional Development
- ♦ Leadership
- ♦ Partnership Development
- ♦ Continuous Improvement and Evaluation

Parallel Readings: Bibliography

The texts below are more recent examples of shared knowledge that will most certainly be helpful to all leaders and participants in school improvement processes. In my own research on school improvement I have often found good practices and strong examples in fields seemingly removed from education, such as in the health care profession and business.

Collins, James C., (2001) *Good to Great: Why some Companies Make the Leap*, New York; Harper Business (ISBN 0-06-662099-6). A great book with lots of things to think about and connect with root cause. The text is based upon five years of study and research on companies that made the leap from good to great and those that did not. Text contains many findings applicable to schools. Check out the website listed below for more specific material and information. http://www.goodtogreatbook.com/

Friedman, Thomas L., (2005) *The World is Flat: A Brief History of the Twenty-First Century*, New York; Farrar, Straus and Giroux (ISBN 0-374-29288-4). A detailed overview of how the world is transforming itself via electronic media and the development of undeveloped countries. In many ways *The World is Flat* is an update on *Future Shock* by Toffler. Check out the following website for more information and detail: http://www.battelleforkids.com/home/flatworld

Giuliani, Rudolph W., (2002) *Leadership*, New York; Hyperion (ISBN: 0786870699). This book provides great insight into how Mayor Giuliani cleaned up New York City and reduced crime and improved social services and prisons through the effective use of data.

Slater, Robert, (1998) *Jack Welch and the G.E. Way*,New York; McGraw-Hill (ISBN 0-07-058104-5). A detailed look at how Jack Welch revolutionized G.E. with echoes of both *Good to Great* and *The World is Flat*. Book provides an interesting insight into G.E. which can be used in the process of school improvement.

Tutorials

Databased Decision Making

Data Pathways

Value-Added Analysis

Systems Thinking

Key Indicators of Student Success

Variation

Root Cause Analysis

Dynamic Planning

The "Quick Tutorials" on the following pages are a means of providing a single page summary of the more important points on each of the topics listed. They might find use in the delivery of training sessions or as a tool for individual "refreshing" following such sessions. Perhaps they can be used as constant reminders of key ideas when kept in proximity to active planning work documents.

A Quick Tutorial on
Databased Decision Making

What Is a DBDM?

DBDM is a system of deeply rooted beliefs, actions, and processes that infuses organizational culture and regularly organizes and transforms data to wisdom for the purpose of making organizational decisions.

Although DBDM can and should be used in all areas of decision making, in schools its importance is in the improvement of student learning.

Why Use DBDM?

1. It is a superior means of making decisions.
2. It requires thought rather than reaction to opinion.
3. It reduces "Akrasia," defined as: engaging in high-risk behavior [not using data] when much safer behavior [using data] is available)
4. The DBDM process transforms data to wisdom.
5. Provides rationale for identification of root cause.
6. Provides rationale for selection of intervention strategy.

What Kinds of Data are Used?

Dr. Victoria Bernhardt has identified the following four measures of data that combine in a great multiple of ways to illuminate what is taking place within the school:

Perceptive Data	Achievement Data
Demographic Data	Process Data

How Is Data Used?

Data, when converted to information, knowledge, understanding, and wisdom is used to:

♦ Monitor Key Indicators of Student Success

♦ Identify problem areas in need of improvement

- Identify root cause(s) of problem areas
- Select intervention strategies aimed at dissolving the root causes
- Monitor implementation and action plans
- Evaluate intervention strategies impact
- Learn about the school system
- Benchmark the school system with itself, others and against standards
- Inform
- Make decisions

A Quick Tutorial on
Data Pathways

What are Data Pathways?

The term "Data Pathways" is a metaphor for the four possible investigative routes that should be taken when converting data to information to knowledge to understanding to wisdom and in seeking root cause. Each of these *pathways* also contains several "lanes."

What are the Four Pathways?

1. The student pathway
2. The System or Organizational Pathway
3. The Benchmarking Pathway
4. The Assessment Pathway

What are the "Lanes"?

1. The Student Pathway
   - The Individual Student Lane
   - Cohorts of Students Lanes
2. The System Pathway
   - The District Lane(s)
   - The Building(s)
   - GradelLevel Lanes
   - The Classroom Lanes
   - Department Lanes
   - Program Lanes
3. The Benchmarking Pathway
   - With self over time Lane
   - With similar schools Lane
   - With the standards Lanes
4. The Assessments

- There will be as many lanes as there are assessments

What Is the Relationship Between Dr. Bernhardt's Multiple Measures of Data and the Data Pathways?

Both models can be used to better understand the process of converting data to wisdom. Neither excludes the other. They can be used separately or together. The whole purpose of both models is to demonstrate how individual pieces of data must be used in conjunction with other pieces of data in order to convert data to wisdom.

A Quick Tutorial on
Value-Added Analysis

What Is Value-Added Analysis?

Value-added analysis is a statistical technique that makes use of student achievement data over time, and screens out non-school variables in order to compute the school's influence upon student progress over time.

Why Use VAA?

VAA provides the "power of two." While schools for some time have used student achievement scores, they have not had the ability to examine student progress absent outside influences.

In some instances, low student progress is masked by high student achievement scores. In other instances, low student achievement scores mask high progress.

To *fully* understand what is taking place in school one

needs to know both student achievement and student progress data.

How Can VAA Help to Improve Schools?

The most immediate result in using VAA is to identify those places where students are not progressing. VAA has the ability to identify this down to the building and classroom level and/or student level.

Once this identification takes place, the next step is to seek cause. Once cause is located, strategies for dissolving the cause must be selected and implemented.

Once implementation is started, monitoring of the implementation process must begin and then evaluation of results takes place: Ddid the strategy do what we hoped it would do? If not, why not?

Where Does VAA fit into DBDM and Dynamic Planning?

Value-added analysis is one more tool in the arsenal of Databased Decision Making and Dynamic Planning. It provides the vital "power of two" by enhancing regular achievement data with progress data.

A Quick Tutorial on
Systems Thinking

What is a System?

A simple system consists of three parts: some form of input, a process, and some form of output. When one has defined these three items, one has defined the system. "Yet… a system is not the sum of its parts, but rather the product of the interaction of the parts!" (Russell Ackoff)

Systems nest within systems: leaf / tree / forest or Class / School Building / School District.

System is defined as "an assemblage or combination of parts forming a complex or unitary whole."

What is Systems Thinking?

♦ Systems thinking is about seeing the whole.

♦ Systems thinkers believe structure influences behavior.

♦ The output of a system is primarily influenced by its processes rather than by individuals. (85%, Deming)

♦ Systems thinking focuses on root causes for problems, not symptoms, and the behaviors flowing from assumptions, and beliefs and the structures shaped by them.

Systems Thoughts

1. A system is a set of parts.
2. Each part affects all other parts.
3. No part has an independent effect on the whole.
4. If you put parts together into a subset, then both 1 and 2 above prevail.

The system is a whole that cannot be divided into independent parts: a car, your hand, your tongue. When a system is taken apart it loses its essential properties.

"We must give up the search for one best educational system, one that operates optimally regardless of time, place, and students. What is required is a system that can learn in, and adapt to, the conditions under which it must operate." (Ackoff)

"The problems of education are not out there in society or the culture—they're in the heads of the people in this room—and we have to break out of our own self-imposed constraints." (Ackoff)

"Fundamental to improvement of schools is the enablement of their functioning as a system rather than as a collection of "school parts." This requires the formation of linkages among the parts in such a manner that all parts perform in harmony with each other and with the goals of the system." (Preuss)

A Quick Tutorial on
Variation

What Is Variation?

Variation is any deviation from the norm. All processes vary. All systems vary. Precision is the result of a very small degree of variation. Variation is the enemy of quality. Variation is expensive.

Why Is Variation Important?

An understanding of variation is essential for the proper use of data. Test scores can vary from year to year simply as a function of normal variation. The smaller the number of students in the cohort, the greater the potential for normal variation. There is a relationship between system improvement and reducing variation.

Understanding variation within your school system, and its sources, is an essential step in working to improve the system.

What Kinds of Variation Occur?

Basically there are two types: common cause variation and special cause variation. Common cause variation is the normal variation that occurs within any process. Special cause variation is the result of some sort of special, infrequent event or circumstance that is typically outside of the normal process. Special cause variation must be eliminated before common cause variation can be reduced. Processes with special cause variation are said "not to be in control." Control does not mean conformity to standards, it just means that there is a certain level of predictability and consistency in results. A process in control may have either consistently good or consistently poor results.

What Tools are Used to Measure Variation?

Although there are many statistical tools that measure variation within numerical data, such as Standard Deviation, Statistical Process Control (SPC) formulas enable the differentiation between common cause variation and special cause variation. Control Charts are used to show process data and the upper and lower limits of control for any process.

A Quick Tutorial on
Key Indicators of Success

What Is a Key Indicator?

A *Key Indicator of Student Success* is a student-focused measurable result that the school has the ability, desire, or need to influence and for which it is willing, or required, to be held accountable.

The concept of key indicators can also be used in other areas of school district organization, such as finances, staffing, instruction, etc.

Why Use Key Indicators?

- KIs make standards both visible and measurable.

- KIs enable measurement of school effectiveness.

- KIs define the purpose of school in measurable terms.

- KIs clarify which data is important and needs analysis.

- KIs enable focused school improvement efforts.

What Drives Key Indicators'?

Key indicators are driven by: district vision, mission, values, and beliefs, and required state and national student standards.

What Do Key Indicators' Drive?

Key Indicators should drive:

- Curriculum and Instruction

- Materials, Methods, Content, Resources

- Comprehensive Planning

- Budget / Staff / Programs / Processes

- Formative and Summative Assessment

Examples of Key Indicators

graduation rates

promotion rates

retention rates

dropout rates

attendance rates

percent of students successfully
    completing a specified sequence of
    courses

International Baccalaureate

achieving scores on ACT/SAT

other exams

grading-distribution rates

Examples of How Key Indicators are Used

Key Indicator	Student Graduation Rate
Desired Ideal Condition	100% of entering ninth-grade cohort will ultimately receive a high school diploma
Present Condition	84% of entering ninth-grade cohort receives a high school diploma
Gap	16% of entering ninth-grade cohort does not receive a diploma
Is this a Priority Issue?	YES!
Goal Statement	Over the course of the next four–year period the percentage of the ninth-grade cohort graduating with a diploma will increase from 84% to 100%.

Search for Root Cause

Selection of Strategies for Improvement

Implementation of Strategies

Monitoring and Evaluation

Key Indicator Planning Template

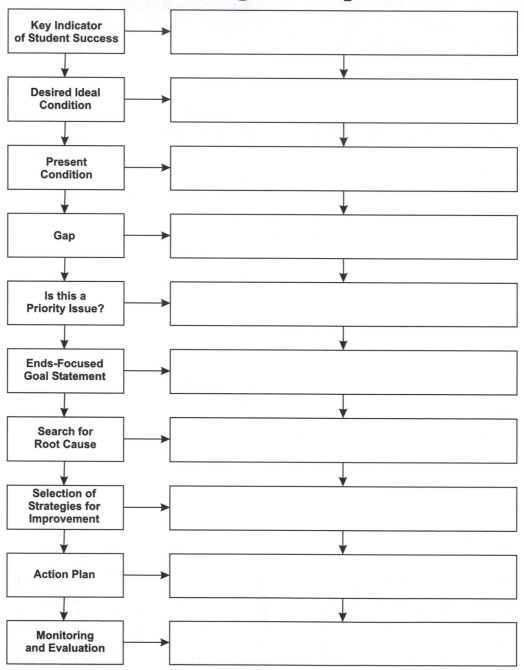

This template may be copied and used as a "shorthand" graphic overview of the planning stemming from a single Key Indicator of Student Success.

Key Indicator Template

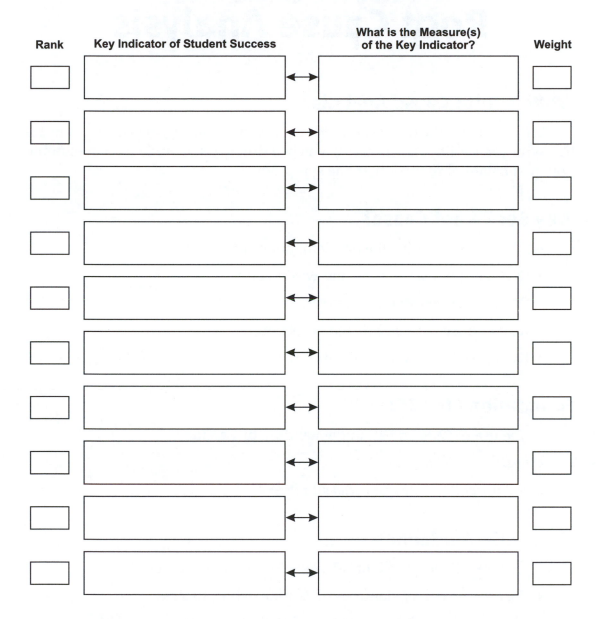

Rank	Key Indicator of Student Success	What is the Measure(s) of the Key Indicator?	Weight

This template can be used when developing Key Indicators of Student Success. It can be given to group participants to consider individually prior to coming to the meeting and it can be used during the meeting to record group decisions as well as group weighting of various Key Indicators. Weighting can be accomplished using a Pareto Process, asking participants to rank highest priority items with a "5," middle priority items with a "3," and lower priority items with a "1." Totals from the whole group are then used to establish rank of the KISS. A form such as this can also be used to communicate the results of meeting with various constituancies and for purposes of verification and feedback.

A Quick Tutorial on
Root Cause Analysis

What Is Root Cause Analysis?

A *Root Cause* is the deepest underlying cause, or causes, of positive or negative symptoms within any process, which, if dissolved, would result in elimination or substantial reduction, of the symptom.

Why Seek Root Cause?

♦ RCA helps dissolve the problem, not just the symptom.

♦ RCA eliminates patching and wasted effort.

♦ RCA conserves scarce resources.

♦ RCA induces discussion and reflection.

♦ RCA provides rationale for strategy selection.

Foundations for RCA

♦ The use of *Data* and an understanding of *Variation*

♦ *Systems Thinking*

♦ *The use of Key Indicators Student Success*

The 4 RCA Modalities

♦ Negative Reactive: identifies roots for existing problems

♦ Positive Reactive: identifies roots for existing success

♦ Negative Proactive: seeks roots for future problems

♦ Positive Proactive: seeks roots for future success

Levels of Root Cause

♦ The incident or procedural level

♦ The programmatic or process level

◆ The systemic level

◆ The external Level

It is important not to make an "incident" into a systemic issue or to treat a systemic issue simply as a bunch of incidents.

RCA Tools

◆ The Questioning Data Process

◆ The Diagnostic Tree Process

◆ The Creative Root Cause Analysis Team Process

◆ The Five Whys

◆ Force Field Analysis

◆ Barrier Analysis

Root cause analysis can be used to seek dissolution of any type of problem (academic, financial, organizational, process) at any level within a school (district, building, program, class, student). It is most effective, however, when used within the context of the whole system as roots are often found far from the problem.

A Quick Tutorial on
Dynamic Planning

What Is Dynamic Planning?

Dynamic Planning is an inclusive, continuous, databased process that creates linkages among all other school system processes, focuses them on improvement of key indicators of student success, and becomes the primary agenda by which the school system organizes its work.

Why Use DP?

Implementation of Dynamic Planning helps to:

◆ Focus school work on Key Indicators of Student Success;

◆ Meet the need for dynamic school reaction in today's dynamic world;

◆ Integrate planning into the daily work of the school;

◆ Quickly identify problems and their root causes in order to identify and implement strategies for their dissolution;

◆ Link all Databased Decision Making processes within the school district and focus them on priority goals.

What are the Four Stages of DP?

The four stages of Dynamic Planning are:

◆ The Adoption Stage

◆ The Implementation Stage

◆ The Expansion Stage

◆ The Optimizing Stage

What are Some of the Requirements
of a Successful Dynamic Planning process?

1. Administrative leadership and commitment

2. Understanding of dynamic planning
3. Widespread Databased Decision Making
4. Data warehousing and querying infrastructure
5. Systems thinking (and acting)
6. Use of root cause analysis
7. Development and use of key indicators of student success
8. Allocation of necessary resources

This listing is not sequential, nor totally complete. Rather it is an outline of key elements that are required for Dynamic Planning to become successful at the Expansion and Optimizing stages. Think of these elements as a system of interrelated parts, each being necessary for the success of both the others and for the whole.

Dynamic Planning: District Commitment Rating Scale

	Deficient / Low ↔ ↔ Effective / High	
Leadership: Key organizational leaders, including the superintendent, are committed to Dynamic Planning and "walking the talk."	1 2 3 4 5 6 7 8	Rating x 2 = ____
Assignment of Resources: Adequate resources (time, money, space, personnel, support) are assigned to the Dynamic Planning process.	1 2 3 4 5 6 7 8	Rating x 1 = ____
Constancy of Purpose: Leaders and organization do not waiver over time in commitment to the Dynamic Planning process.	1 2 3 4 5 6 7 8	Rating x 1 = ____
Focus on Student Results: The primary focus of Dynamic Planning efforts is on improved learning for all students.	1 2 3 4 5 6 7 8	Rating x 1 = ____
Sincerity of Effort: Dynamic Planning is seen as an honest effort to improve learning for all students — not something driven only by mandate, not a paper chase.	1 2 3 4 5 6 7 8	Rating x 1 = ____
Hard Work: It is evident that those leading and those involved in the effort have committed, or are willing to commit, significant amounts of energy to Dynamic Planning.	1 2 3 4 5 6 7 8	Rating x 1 = ____
Integration within System: Dynamic Planning is "open" and links to all aspects of the school organization. This is not a "sidecar" effort.	1 2 3 4 5 6 7 8	Rating x 1 = ____
Involvement of Stakeholders: A wide variety of stakeholders have been encouraged and have joined the effort.	1 2 3 4 5 6 7 8	Rating x 1 = ____
Organizational Buy-In: A significant number within major stakeholder groups have "bought into" and support Dynamic Planning.	1 2 3 4 5 6 7 8	Rating x 1 = ____

Add all 9 sub-scores: Total = ____

Divide by 10 to obtain final Commitment Score: ____

Dynamic Planning: District Capacity Rating Scale

Deficient / Low ◄———► Effective / High

Understanding of the process: Leaders, team members, and a good number of stakeholders understand the basic concept and purpose of the Dynamic Planning.

1 2 3 4 5 6 7 8   Rating x 2 = ____

Technical Skills: Leaders, team members, and a good number of staff understand and can use basic concepts such as systems thinking, data and root cause analysis, key indicators of student success, and databased decision making.

1 2 3 4 5 6 7 8   Rating x 2 = ____

Dynamic Planning: DP is well integrated and is used regularly as the organizational framework for the ongoing work of the school.

1 2 3 4 5 6 7 8   Rating x 1 = ____

Distributed Leadership: Leadership is distributed throughout the organization depending upon task.

1 2 3 4 5 6 7 8   Rating x 1 = ____

Communication: An open communication process has been established and is used effectively to keep all stakeholders and other school processes informed and involved. (Linkages)

1 2 3 4 5 6 7 8   Rating x 1 = ____

Data: Essential data on key indicators of student success is available and in a form that can easily be used for analysis.

1 2 3 4 5 6 7 8   Rating x 1 = ____

Implementation: Detailed and specific implementation plans are created for all activities and strategies and kept up-to-date.

1 2 3 4 5 6 7 8   Rating x 1 = ____

Monitoring and Evaluation: Dynamic Planning is constantly monitored and results are evaluated on a continuous basis.

1 2 3 4 5 6 7 8   Rating x 1 = ____

Organizational Learning: The organization is committed to continuous learning in pursuit of improved learning for all students.

1 2 3 4 5 6 7 8   Rating x 1 = ____

Trust: There is a high degree of trust among participants in the improvement process.

1 2 3 4 5 6 7 8   Rating x 1 = ____

Add all 10 sub-scores: Total = ____

Divide by 12 to obtain final Capacity Score: ____

District Commitment/Capacity Scale

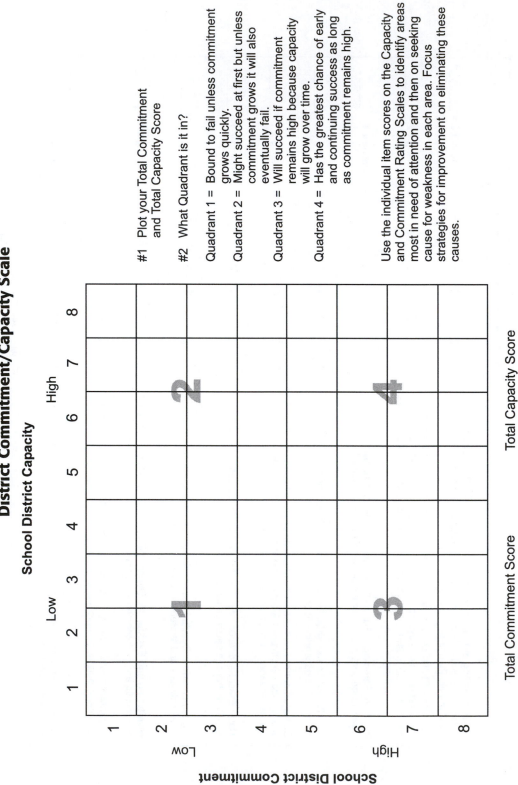

School District Capacity

Low   High

1   2   3   4   5   6   7   8

School District Commitment

Low   High

1   2   3   4   5   6   7   8

Total Commitment Score _____

Total Capacity Score _____

#1 Plot your Total Commitment and Total Capacity Score

#2 What Quadrant is it in?

Quadrant 1 = Bound to fail unless commitment grows quickly.

Quadrant 2 = Might succeed at first but unless commitment grows it will also eventually fail.

Quadrant 3 = Will succeed if commitment remains high because capacity will grow over time.

Quadrant 4 = Has the greatest chance of early and continuing success as long as commitment remains high.

Use the individual item scores on the Capacity and Commitment Rating Scales to identify areas most in need of attention and then on seeking cause for weakness in each area. Focus strategies for improvement on eliminating these causes.